"The cross stands tall at the center of the gospel. Mike writes with an earthy, pastoral voice and a deep understanding of the drama and beauty of Jesus' crucifixion. Thoroughly rooted in the gospel, *Passion* draws us back again and again to reflect on its truths."
Daniel Montgomery, Founder and Lead Pastor of Sojourn Community Church, Louisville, Kentucky

"This is a gripping explanation of the crucifixion which gets right to the heart of the death of Jesus. It is clear, challenging, heartwarming and practical."
William Taylor, Rector of St Helen's Bishopsgate, London

"This book takes us deep into the Lord Jesus and deep into His atoning work. Mike McKinley's exploration of Christ's Passion is electric in its surprising connections to the Old Testament and exhilariting in its applictions of the cross to life today."
Gene Veith, Professor of Literature and Provost, Patrick Henry College, Virginia

"*Passion* wipes the dust off the familiar events of Christ's last day, showing just what a difference the cross makes to everyday life. Warning: Mike's insights are like nails!"
Michael Reeves, author of "Delighting in the Trinity" (US) / "The Good God" (UK); Head of Theology at UCCF, UK

"This is a readable and attractive way into Luke's account of the crucifixion and resurrection of Jesus Christ. Mike McKinley helps us understand what happened, what it meant, and what it means for us today. A moving book which will enrich and challenge anyone who reads it."
Peter Adam, former principal of Ridley College, Melbourne; author of "Written for Us"

"I hope many will read and absorb this book. It offers a sweet series of meditations on Jesus Christ's life-changing and universe-altering final day. It is an excellent read for both seeker and Christian."
Jonathan Leeman, Editorial Director of 9Marks Ministries; author of "Reverberation" and "The Surprising Offense of God's Love"

"Mike McKinley writes with a warm, easy style, explaining Luke's account of the Passion clearly and showing us how, so often, our hearts are the same as those who Jesus met and spoke to on that day. As I read I found I was moved to marvel afresh at the beauty of the Saviour and the magnitude of His love."
Andrea Trevenna, women's worker at St Nicholas Sevenoaks, Kent; author of "The Heart of Singleness"

"These reflections from Luke's Gospel left me in awe of the glory of Christ: broken by His sacrifice, warmed by His love, and inspired by His example. *Passion* is packed with biblical insights, devotional thoughts, and useful application. Prepare to be changed by the power of the cross."
Jared Mellinger, senior pastor of Covenant Fellowship Church, Glen Mills, Pennsylvania

"Here is a faithful, fresh and insightful perspective on the gospel story. It connects the climactic moments of Jesus' life to the everyday events of our own, and encourages us to look in the mirror at our lives in the light of His."
Paul Perkin, senior pastor of St Mark's Battersea Rise, London and regular New Wine speaker

"This is a compelling portrait of Jesus, history's central person. I frequently found myself needing to put the book to one side so that I could worship and thank God for a wonderful Savior."
Sam Allberry, author of "Connected" and "Lifted"; Associate Minister of St Mary's Maidenhead, UK

"Beautifully simple, stunningly insightful, unswervingly biblical and compellingly practical. Chapter by chapter, I was confronted by fresh glimpses of the gospel of grace and challenged to live a cross-shaped life in response. Wherever you're at with Jesus, this superb book will do your soul good.
Dai Hankey, pastor of Hill City Church, south Wales; author of "The Hard Corps"

"Mike McKinley has captured, simply and beautifully, the depths and riches of the last hours and death of Jesus. Here we are presented with nothing but Jesus Christ, and Him crucified, which is why this book was such a joy to read."
John Hindley, pastor of BroadGrace Church, Norfolk, UK; author of "Serving Without Sinking"

MIKE McKINLEY

PASSION

HOW CHRIST'S FINAL DAY
CHANGES YOUR EVERY DAY

About the author

Mike McKinley is Pastor of Guilford Baptist Church in Sterling, Virginia. He is married to Karen, and they have five children. Mike received his MDiv from Westminster Theological Seminary, Philadelphia, and is author of *Am I Really a Christian?* and *Church Planting is for Wimps*.

To Kendall, Knox, Phineas, Ebenezer and Harper.
May this be the story that shapes your lives.

Passion: *How Christ's final day changes your every day*
© Michael McKinley/The Good Book Company, 2013

Published by
The Good Book Company
Tel (UK): 0333 123 0880;
International: +44 (0) 208 942 0880
Email: admin@thegoodbook.co.uk

Websites:
N America: www.thegoodbook.com
UK: www.thegoodbook.co.uk
Australia: www.thegoodbook.com.au
New Zealand: www.thegoodbook.co.nz

the good book
COMPANY

ISBN (US): 9781908762580
ISBN (ROW): 9781908762061

Printed and bound by CPI Group (UK) Ltd, Croydon, CR0 4YY
Design by André Parker

CONTENTS

INTRODUCTION

PAST, FUTURE AND PRESENT

What difference does the cross of Jesus Christ make to the way you live?

For many people, the answer to that question is simple: no difference at all. It's a mere fact of history, no more life-changing than the death of Socrates, or Martin Luther King, or any other innocent man. Most human beings live, work, raise their families, grow old, and finally die without being in any way influenced by the fact that Jesus of Nazareth was crucified on a hill outside Jerusalem 2,000 years ago.

Christians, of course, answer differently. Christians hold that the crucifixion of Christ is the center of human history, because on the cross Jesus died for their sins to secure life beyond death for His followers. Christians are banking their eternal destiny on this one event. Because Jesus died, they have a certain hope of eternal life with God.

But it seems to me that many Christians are still missing something important when they think about the cross. We tend to think about the final hours of Jesus' life *only* in terms of the future, in terms of our eternal destiny. We can treat the cross like a ticket to an evening football game that we're carrying around in our pocket. We're really excited about it, we're grateful for it, but we won't need it until we get to the stadium. We can think that the cross is great, and we'll definitely need it when we die... and that's about it.

But what about those seventy (or so) years that we live before we enter into eternity? Does the death of Christ make any difference for these years, the here and now? Does it give us anything *more* than the future hope of heaven?

The answer of the writers of the New Testament is a resounding "Yes!". For them, the cross didn't change only the future, but also everything about the present. It's actually a bit surprising how they keep placing sweeping teaching about the cosmic significance of Jesus' suffering and death right next to very practical application about how we should live our lives today (have a look, for instance, at Philippians 2 v 3-8).

The cross of Christ is the reality that gives shape to the way Christians should think about every detail of our lives right now, from our marriages to our money, from our suffering to our success.

So this is a book about a past event, a single day in a single man's life. But because that single day is the final day of Jesus' earthly life, it's a book that is all about the future, too. And it's still more than that. As we look at what is often called Christ's "Passion" through the eyes of Luke's Gospel, we'll encounter almost every conceivable human emotion and character quality. We'll have much to learn from the cowardice of Peter and Pilate, and from the bravery of Joseph of Arimathea. The devotion of the women who stayed with Jesus to the very end will encourage us, just as the treachery of Judas will warn us. And ultimately, the words and actions of Jesus over the course of the hardest day of His life will model for us what it means to live faithful lives in the middle of a broken world.

In other words, this book is about the present. It's about today, and how Christ's final day transforms our every day. The more I read the Passion narratives in the Gospels, the more I'm convinced that there are no wasted words, spare characters or unimportant moments. Each is there, as we'll see, to teach us. Each of the moments Luke (inspired by God's Spirit) relates to us has a purpose for our lives *today*.

The cross of Christ is all we will need, and all we will have, on the last day of this life. But wonderfully, it's also all that we need for today, and tomorrow, and every day up till that last one.

There are many wonderful books on the cross of Christ, and it won't take you long to figure out that this one is not meant to provide a definitive word on the subject. No book can—Christians will spend an eternity being amazed by what happened on that day 2,000 years ago.

But this book *is* intended to change the way you live and dream—not because of this book itself, but because of the events it points you to. At the end of each chapter, you'll find a few questions to help you think through what you've read, as well as a hymn or poem to assist you in meditating on the Bible truths you've been looking at.

If you are a new believer, I hope that this book will help you better understand and appreciate and be stirred by the cross. If you're a long-standing Christian, I'd love it if this book helped you work out more of the way that the Lord's final hours before His death impact your daily life. And if you're not yet a follower of Jesus, it's my prayer that God would use this book as a means of opening your eyes to the most wonderful news imaginable.

Whoever you are, I'm praying that Jesus' Passion will inspire your passion for Him, and that you'll be able to say with great confidence and excitement once you've finished:

To me, to live is Christ and to die is gain.

(Philippians 1 v 21)

CHAPTER ONE

THE CUP

³⁹ Jesus went out as usual to the Mount of Olives, and his disciples followed him. ⁴⁰ On reaching the place, he said to them, "Pray that you will not fall into temptation." ⁴¹ He withdrew about a stone's throw beyond them, knelt down and prayed, ⁴² "Father, if you are willing, take this cup from me; yet not my will, but yours be done." ⁴³ An angel from heaven appeared to him and strengthened him. ⁴⁴ And being in anguish, he prayed more earnestly, and his sweat was like drops of blood falling to the ground. ⁴⁵ When he rose from prayer and went back to the disciples, he found them asleep, exhausted from sorrow. ⁴⁶ "Why are you sleeping?" he asked them. "Get up and pray so that you will not fall into temptation."

Luke 22 v 39-46

Imagine that one day you're hurrying along the street, with a thousand things on your mind and on your to-do list, when you see a good friend sitting on a bench some distance away. You haven't seen them in a while, and you smile as you realize it's them.

But as you come closer, you begin to sense that something's wrong. The smile that you thought you saw on their face is actually a grimace. Their eyes contain tears, and their back is slumped. They seem overwhelmed by sadness and anguish.

How would you respond? I'd like to think that I would drop everything, forget my schedule, and run to my friend.

I'd want to know what was wrong. I'd want to take time to listen to them, to understand my friend's suffering.

Luke's painting of this scene on a hillside, the night before Good Friday begins, presents us with something a little bit like that scenario. We are coming across Jesus in a moment of "anguish" (v 44). Now, if you know anything about Jesus, you probably know that He was not an emotionally fragile man. He was fearless and compassionate, strong and tender. But not here. Here He seems almost broken.

How will you respond? Let's drop everything, forget the other thoughts in our heads, and listen to Him. Let's take time to understand and appreciate what is wrong; why this strongest of men is on His knees, sweating as He prays.

But first, let's set the scene.

A Man Like No Other

We're jumping into the middle (well, actually, almost the end) of a story, or in many ways a biography. So as we watch Jesus on the Mount of Olives on that dark night, it's well worth seeing how He got there.

The author of the book of Luke is a man named Luke (whoever came up with the title clearly wasn't blessed with much imagination), a physician and amateur historian who lived in the time of Jesus. As far as we know, Luke didn't know Jesus personally or witness any of the things that he records in his biography of the Lord. Instead, he tells us (1 v 1-4) that he carefully researched the events surrounding Jesus' birth, life, ministry, death, resurrection, and ascension into heaven.

In the first twenty two-and-a-half chapters of his Gospel, Luke has shown us that Jesus is a man like no other; in fact, that He is the Son of God. We've seen Jesus call together a motley band of disciples, teach the masses about the salvation He would bring, perform many healings and miracles, and predict His own death and resurrection. Then, on this particular night, as Jesus celebrates the Passover meal with His friends for the last time, He reveals that He knows that one of His disciples, Judas Iscariot, has agreed to betray the Lord into the hands of His jealous rivals. The stage is set for the most difficult night of Jesus' life.

After leaving the Passover meal, Jesus goes with His disciples to the Mount of Olives (22 v 39), a quiet place He went to frequently. Matthew and Mark's accounts of Jesus' life tell us that He stops in the Garden of Gethsemane, a secluded retreat on the hillside. There He leaves them, twice instructing them that they should use the time to pray that they would not fall into temptation (v 40).

But instead of praying, they fall asleep "from sorrow" (v 45). It seems that they are simply emotionally and physically drained. At the very moment that Jesus most needed His friends' love and support and prayers, they fall asleep. And sadly, I can relate to the misplaced priorities of the disciples here. When life is overwhelming, I often find it easier to sleep than to pray.

The bustle of the meal is left far behind; even His closest friends are asleep; and whatever Jesus is about to experience, He will go through it completely alone.

Deep Anguish

Jesus goes a little way away to pray (v 41). Throughout Luke, we're told of Jesus praying to His heavenly Father. Prayer was the way that Jesus prepared for big challenges and recovered from the difficulties of His ministry. When something important was about to happen, Jesus prayed. When the crowds were pressing in on Him, Jesus would still find time to pray. Now, Jesus knows that He has been betrayed. He knows that His arrest is not far off. So we would expect Jesus to go to His Father for comfort, strength, and renewal.

But instead of finding peace in prayer, Jesus begins to experience something terrible, so much so that an angel has to be sent to strengthen Him (v 43). Luke tells us that He is in agony, experiencing such anguish (mental? physical? spiritual? all three?) that His sweat is like blood. The picture painted for us is one of a person in total "system overload"; Jesus' physical body and human nature can barely endure what is happening.

The Cup

So we have to ask: what could possibly cause *this* kind of agony to *this* kind of man?

We can say with certainty that Jesus is not merely caving into fear as He anticipates dying. It cannot possibly be that Jesus is a coward, undone by the certainty of His own death. After all, Jesus has been speaking about His crucifixion for some time. He's deliberately walked towards the city where He knew it would happen. The cause of Jesus' turmoil in the garden can't be a straightforward fear of death. There must be something more going on.

And verse 42 reveals that there is. "Father," Jesus prays, "if you are willing, take this cup from me." Mark and Matthew's Gospels tell us that Jesus cried out three separate times for relief from "this cup". The source of Jesus' anguish is a *cup*. What cup could possibly cause this kind of agony?

A look at a couple of Old Testament passages sheds some light on it. The prophets of Israel sometimes spoke of God's wrath and judgment against sin as a "cup" that the wicked were required to drink. And so the prophet Isaiah wrote to the people of Jerusalem, whose city had been sacked and who had been carried off by the Babylonian armies:

> Awake, awake! Rise up, O Jerusalem, you who have drunk from the hand of the LORD the cup of his wrath, you who have drained to its dregs the goblet that makes men stagger. (Isaiah 51 v 17)

And in the same way, God told the prophet Jeremiah about the disaster He was sending to the nations around Israel:

> This is what the LORD, the God of Israel, said to me: "Take from my hand this cup filled with the wine of my wrath and make all the nations to whom I send you drink it. When they drink it, they will stagger and go mad because of the sword I will send among them."
> (Jeremiah 25 v 15-16)

In the Old Testament, "the cup" is symbolic. It represents the fury, anger and punishment of God. To put it simply, "the cup" is full of God's perfect and holy hatred for sin. And here on the mountainside, Jesus begins to taste what is in that cup, unmingled and undiluted by God's mercy.

The Wrath

Now, allow me to anticipate an objection at this point. Perhaps you are thinking to yourself something along the lines of: "Wrath? Really? Is that the kind of God I'm supposed to love? I expect wrath and fury from a spoiled toddler, not the Almighty God of the universe!" Maybe that thought has occurred to you; if not, you've probably heard someone else give voice to it.

And so before we go any further, it's worth taking a significant detour and addressing the issue of God's wrath.

If the Bible showed us that God's anger against sin is like the fury of a badly-behaved child, then we would have a problem. It would be hard to respect or love or trust God if He were like that. But the Bible describes God's wrath as something that is actually part of His perfection—not a suspension of it. It is an expression of His holiness and His hatred for wickedness.

In fact, God wouldn't be God if He were not willing to punish sin and injustice. If God were *not* a God of wrath, we should not respect, or love or trust Him.

I realize that might be a controversial statement for some, so let's take it out on the road for a test drive. Because if perfect wrath is part of God's holy character, then we might rightly expect it to show up in the noble character of humanity, right? The Bible teaches that humans are made in God's image, that we reflect something of His character and intelligence. And so if God is rightly wrathful, then we would expect that would show up at times when human beings are at their very best.

A friend of mine recently told me about a time in an east Asian nation where his hosts drove him into the capital city. As they entered the city, they were confronted by a long line of young girls, lined up by the side of the road. These girls had been sold into slavery as prostitutes (often by their parents), and they would spend their lives being used and abused until they were finally cast aside when they were no longer desirable. My friend described his feelings as he saw these girls: an anger, a rage in his heart that made him feel as if his chest was going to rip in two.

Was my friend's anger good? Was it right and pure? Or should he have thought about the parents who had sold these innocent girls, the men who had pimped them, and the "clients" who had abused them, with a sort of smiling, indifferent benevolence? Should you? Of course not! Anger in the face of brutal oppression is a good and right thing.

If that goes for humans, it goes for the God who made humans, too. God's hatred for sin is *part* of His perfection. The Bible tells us so... and deep in our hearts we know it ought to be so. Those girls lined up along the roadside are just a drop in the total bucket of human evil. They represent just the evil being done in one small place on one day. But now begin to add up the totality of injustice done in all of human history (genocide, chattel slavery, racism, oppression). We simply can't have a good God who doesn't hate sin and who won't do something about it someday.

But where we really run into a problem, where we really object to God's wrath and justice, is when it comes to *us*. We may be happy with a God who punishes the rapists and the murderers, but we aren't happy with a God who punishes us. But where would you have God draw the line? How much should He tolerate from you? How much of your pride, anger, deceit, manipulation and selfishness do you think God should overlook?

The Bible tells us where God draws the line: He demands perfection. God is perfectly holy and He created us to obey Him perfectly, and He will not lie and say that your sin and my sin is not a big deal. We all deserve God's wrath.

A God who is committed to justice is good news for us as sufferers, but it is terrifying news for us as sinners. That cup of wrath fits naturally in my hands, in your hands, and in the hands of every human alive.

The First Sip

Now we're ready to wrestle with what is happening as Jesus prepares to drink that cup. Jesus Himself has never sinned. He has never earned God's righteous hatred for His wickedness. He is the only person in human history who doesn't deserve to face the wrath of a perfect and holy God. But in this dark night on the Mount of Olives, Jesus begins tasting in His soul the contents of that awful cup. In a few hours, at the cross, He will drain it to its dregs. Why?

So that we wouldn't have to drink any of it, ever.

It's impossible to overstate the magnitude and mystery of this moment. This is an event that remains utterly unique in human history. Stop and think about it: here in the garden, the perfect, sinless, holy Son of God, whose soul recoils at the presence of sin, begins to taste what it will be like to be treated like a sinner, to face wrath like a sinner. Here the Son of God, the second person of the Trinity, who has eternally enjoyed perfect unity and love with His Father, begins to feel what it will be like to be forsaken and abandoned by Him. We cannot hope to fully understand or explain these events. We can only describe them, believe them, and be led to worship by them.

For those of us who have received forgiveness through Jesus' blood, we have here on the Mount of Olives a beautiful picture of our Lord's love for us. Can you imagine what it was like for Jesus to endure the cross? If just a taste, just the anticipation of that wrath, was enough to make Jesus fall to the ground and sweat drops like blood, how much worse was His actual experience at His crucifixion the next day? Why did He do it? So that we would never need to face any of it, ever.

The Representative

And so on that night, in that place, Jesus was acting as our representative.

To grasp the significance of what Jesus is doing here, we need to rewind way back through the storyline of the Bible, to the very beginning. How did sin and death come into the world? God created Adam and Eve, the first humans, and placed them in the Garden of Eden. And in that garden they were given a choice between obedience and disobedience (Genesis 2 v 16-17). If they obeyed God's will, they would experience nothing but the joy and blessing and the peace of God for which they were created. Disobedience, on the other hand, would bring death and wrath. Adam and Eve chose sin and death, and you and I have followed in their footsteps.

Now in your mind's eye fast-forward through the millennia from the Garden of Eden to the Garden of Gethsemane. At every point in His life, Jesus has always obeyed His Father. And here in this garden He has the choice: will He obey the Father, or not? But Jesus' choice is not exactly like the choice that faced Adam. There is an important difference. For Adam, obedience to God meant that he would experience blessing and peace. For Jesus, choosing to obey God means that He will be cursed and crushed. If Jesus obeys the Father's will and goes to the cross, He will experience unimaginable horror.

Which is why the words at the end of verse 42 are some of the most awesome in the entire Bible. Take this cup from me, Jesus begs His Father: "yet not my will, but yours be done".

It's just the opposite of what Adam did. Adam said to God: "My will, not yours!" But Jesus said: "Even though it will cost me everything, let your will be done, not mine". Jesus is doing what Adam did not do. He is doing what we do not do. He is our representative, obeying as we should obey and enduring what we should endure.

Has there ever been a greater act of obedience? Has there ever been a greater act of love to God and neighbor? What an amazing Savior we have. This is why Christians have had to write songs to express the love and adoration we feel for Jesus. Sometimes ordinary words don't seem like enough!

But pausing to look at Jesus on the mountainside doesn't just overflow in our songs, but in our lives. Jesus' highest priority was the will of His heavenly Father, even when it was costly and dangerous. And Jesus tells His followers to pray to their heavenly Father: "Your will be done" (Matthew 6 v 10). We need to realize what we're doing when we say that line in the "Lord's Prayer". We need to realize that obedience to God's will may often be difficult and painful. It's not enough to say those words; we must be willing to live them. Jesus shows us what that means; it means suffering the loss of comfort, convenience, reputation, even our lives.

More than an Example

When we think about what Jesus endured that night for us, we see a wonderful (and challenging) example of how we ought to live. We see that we should pray when we are facing difficulties. We see that we should obey even when we are facing a great cost. As we see Jesus waking up His disciples and encouraging them to pray instead of blasting them for failing to keep Him company, we see that we need to be patient with those who let us down.

Jesus is a fantastic example for us, in fact the best example ever. But if that's all we take away from this passage, we have completely missed the point—because Jesus doesn't kneel there in that garden primarily as your example. If you walk away from these verses thinking that you just need to try harder so that you live like Jesus, you will be absolutely crushed. You cannot do it.

The point of these events is not for you and me to look at Jesus' bravery and His forgiveness and His trust and His sacrifice and be inspired to be a bit more like Him. The point is that you and I should realize that we're *not* like Jesus, that we don't love and forgive and trust and obey the way that we should. We don't just need an inspiring example; we need a saving substitute. We need someone who will take our punishment, and who will give us His perfection. We need someone who will die our death and give us life. We need a Savior. We don't need Jesus to do things better than us, to learn from; we need Jesus to do it for us, to be saved by.

On the Mount of Olives, we see Jesus, under the most extreme circumstances imaginable, tasting the cup of God's wrath. And it staggers Him. It astonishes Him. It knocks Him to the ground. But it doesn't shake His love for you. Not an ounce. If you're a Christian, you can look at Jesus contemplating the cup of hell, surrounded by disciples who are failing Him, and you can see Him saying to His Father: *I will take it for them.*

You are Loved

And so if you're a Christian, you can look at Jesus kneeling in anguish and know beyond all doubt that God loves you. What is going to happen, what is going to change that would make Jesus stop loving you? If the fury of God's holy wrath doesn't do it, what will? If God the Father loved you enough that He would send the Son that He loved to endure this kind of suffering for you, what will shake His love for you? "He who did not spare his own Son, but gave him up for us all—how will he not also, along with him, graciously give us all things?" (Romans 8 v 32).

You may not consider yourself particularly loveable. You may have spent most of your life looking for something or someone to make you feel loved. You may have been burned or betrayed by someone who said "I love you" but proved to mean "I love me". You may have settled for receiving a half-hearted love which is less than you'd dreamed of, but the best you think you'll find. You may have been told that you must learn to love yourself, but deep down that's proving impossible because you can't ignore the un-lovely things that you know about yourself. You may have been laboring under the feeling that you need to get good enough to earn God's love.

Well, look at Jesus on the Mount of Olives, saying to the Father: *I will take the cup.* He took it for you. He loved you so much that He did that for you. You are loved, by the only One in the universe whose love matters eternally. He loves you!

For Reflection:

- *God feels right anger at injustice and sin. How does your heart reflect His? How could it do so more?*
- *Are there areas of your life where you're doing what's easy and disobeying God instead of what's costly in obedience to Him? How does Jesus' example inspire you to change?*
- *When and why do you feel unworthy of love? How will you remind yourself of Jesus' unshakeable love at those moments?*

Oh, what wondrous love I see,
Freely shown for you and me,
By the One who did atone!
Just to show His matchless grace,
Jesus suffered for the race,
In Gethsemane, alone.

Long in anguish deep was He,
Weeping there for you and me.
For God's wrath to Him was known;
We should love Him evermore
For the anguish that He bore
In Gethsemane, alone.

Oh, what love, what matchless love,
Oh, what love for me was shown!
His forever I will be,
For the love He gave to me,
When He suffered all alone.

"In Gethsemane Alone" by Samuel E. Reed

CHAPTER TWO

BETRAYAL AND DENIAL

⁴⁷ While he was still speaking a crowd came up, and the man who was called Judas, one of the Twelve, was leading them. He approached Jesus to kiss him, ⁴⁸ but Jesus asked him, "Judas, are you betraying the Son of Man with a kiss?"

⁴⁹ When Jesus' followers saw what was going to happen, they said, "Lord, should we strike with our swords?" ⁵⁰ And one of them struck the servant of the high priest, cutting off his right ear.

⁵¹ But Jesus answered, "No more of this!" And he touched the man's ear and healed him.

⁵² Then Jesus said to the chief priests, the officers of the temple guard, and the elders, who had come for him, "Am I leading a rebellion, that you have come with swords and clubs? ⁵³ Every day I was with you in the temple courts, and you did not lay a hand on me. But this is your hour—when darkness reigns."

⁵⁴ Then seizing him, they led him away and took him into the house of the high priest. Peter followed at a distance. ⁵⁵ But when they had kindled a fire in the middle of the courtyard and had sat down together, Peter sat down with them. ⁵⁶ A servant girl saw him seated there in the firelight. She looked closely at him and said, "This man was with him."

⁵⁷ But he denied it. "Woman, I don't know him," he said.

⁵⁸ A little later someone else saw him and said, "You also are one of them."

"Man, I am not!" Peter replied.

⁵⁹ About an hour later another asserted, "Certainly this fellow was with him, for he is a Galilean."

⁶⁰ Peter replied, "Man, I don't know what you're talking about!" Just as he was speaking, the cock crowed. ⁶¹ The Lord turned and looked straight at Peter. Then Peter remembered the word the Lord had spoken to him: "Before the cock crows today, you will disown me three times." ⁶² And he went outside and wept bitterly.

Luke 22 v 47-62

Have you ever been hurt by a close friend? Perhaps you shared something with them in confidence, only to have them share it with all your friends. Maybe they'd promised to help you with something very important, but they bailed out at the last minute. Or even worse, perhaps they just rejected you and stopped being your friend at all.

There's something particularly painful about being let down by someone that you trust. It's worse to be wounded by a friend than to be hurt by an enemy.

We are now at the beginning of the end of Jesus' earthly ministry. From this point, Jesus will be in the custody of His enemies. This scene opens with a crowd of people bursting into the quiet of the garden to arrest Him. And Luke tells us in a very matter-of-fact way the most harrowing detail— they were led by someone who was supposed to be Jesus' friend: Judas Iscariot.

Luke has told us earlier in his biography of Jesus that Judas had agreed to betray Jesus to the Jewish religious authorities in exchange for some money (22 v 3-6). Because Jesus was so popular with the people, the religious leaders did not dare to seize Him in public; they had to have a disciple betray Jesus to them when He was far from the crowds. Jesus highlights their cowardice in verse 53, when He asks them why they didn't come for Him in the temple when He was teaching the crowds.

But it's not the leaders who most darken the scene here; it's the man whose name has gone down in history as synonymous with betrayal.

Judas: The Worst Friend?

The main drama of this arrest scene is in the interaction between Judas and Jesus. It's bad enough that Jesus will be arrested and killed; that alone is a horrible injustice. But it is made that much worse by the fact that He is handed over by a man who was supposed to be one of His closest friends, a man who had walked and talked and lived with Jesus for three years!

Surely Judas must qualify as the worst friend ever. On the very night of this betrayal, Jesus had washed Judas' feet and broken bread with him. In the ancient near east, hospitality was a crucial part of life. To break bread with someone was a sign of fellowship and partnership. To sit at the table with someone and then betray him was a hideous breach of decency.

Then in the garden, Judas betrays Jesus with a kiss, turning a sign of friendship into a gesture of treachery. It is as if a friend gave you a hug and planted a knife between your shoulder blades while his arms were around you.

And yet, remarkably, Jesus loves Judas even as he slides the knife in.

In verse 48, Jesus asks him if he is really going to follow through with his plan. Think about that for a second. Is

Jesus trying to get information out of Judas? Of course not! He is being kind, giving Judas one last opportunity to reconsider his plan. Matthew's Gospel tells us that Jesus even called him "friend" (Matthew 26 v 50). But Judas is set on betrayal. He responds to the gentle kindness of Jesus by giving Him that traitor's kiss. It is hard to imagine a worse friend than Judas.

Past Performance is No Guarantee

It's worth remembering the things that Judas had seen and done. He was one of the disciples sent out to preach the gospel, with power to cast out demons and heal people (Luke 9 v 1-2). He sat in a boat as Jesus calmed a storm with a word (8 v 22-25). He saw Jesus feed the 5,000 (9 v 10-17). He watched as Jesus raised people from the dead (7 v 11-17). He heard Jesus' sermons, probably multiple times. He was personally selected by Jesus to be part of His inner circle. He had even had his feet washed by Jesus!

And yet... despite all of those amazing experiences, Judas turns out not to be a disciple. He is not a true follower of Jesus. In the end, he is a traitor and a liar and a thief. He is a real-life example of what Jesus warns in Matthew 7 v 21-23:

> Not everyone who says to me, "Lord, Lord," will enter the kingdom of heaven ... Many will say to me on that day, "Lord, Lord, did we not prophesy in your name, and in your name drive out demons and perform many miracles?" Then I will tell them plainly, "I never knew you!"

Judas is a chilling reminder to us that you can't rely on your past experiences as an indication of your current spiritual condition. And so Judas' example should cause us to pause. If you think of yourself as a Christian, have you ever stopped to think how you can be sure that you really are a Christian? Why are you confident that you are a genuine follower of Jesus? Because your parents are believers? Because you go to a church and everyone there assumes you are a Christian? Because you have served faithfully in your church? Maybe even because you've preached sermons or led people to Christ?

Judas reminds us that nothing you have done in the past can assure you that you are truly a follower of Christ. Yes, good fruit in your life is a good sign. But look at Judas; examine the resumé that he could roll out for you. He looked good on paper, but in reality he sent Jesus to His death. Nothing you or I have seen or accomplished, nothing in our pedigree or experience can ultimately make us a Christian!

Ordinary Betrayal

Judas' impressive past challenges my assumptions; and the nature of Judas' sin does, too. Because what he did was just so *ordinary*.

That seems a strange thing to say, because what Judas did was terrible. Not for nothing did Dante put Judas at the center of his hellish "Inferno". But still, there was something about it that was terribly ordinary.

Back in Luke 22 v 21, Jesus told the disciples that one of them would betray Him; and the disciples had a really weird response. They all began to wonder aloud if it was going to be them. That was totally out of character for the disciples. Usually, they were busy bragging about who was going to be first in the kingdom and telling Jesus all the things they were willing to do for Him. But here, there was something in all of them that made them wonder if *they* were going to be the betrayer.

We don't know exactly why Judas did what he did. But clearly, on some level he was dissatisfied with Jesus. Jesus wasn't what Judas wanted Him to be. And you can bet that all the other disciples were struggling with the same thought. In just the last week, Jesus had ridden into Jerusalem as a King and stood in the temple every day, calling out the religious leaders and cleansing the temple. Tensions were rising. The powers that be were getting angry. Sitting at that last supper, the disciples began to realize that everything was about to go down. There was no going back, but Jesus didn't seem to have any plan to get them out of Jerusalem. Quite the reverse: He kept talking about suffering.

And so they probably had at least a little thought in the back of their mind: when everything comes to a head, how am I going to save my skin? And now, as Jesus is led off, they quietly melt away. None of them will die with Him. They are happy to fight their way out with swords, but not to follow their Master to the cross.

To a degree, all the disciples are struggling with the fact that Jesus isn't who they want Him to be. None of them had decided to follow Jesus because they wanted to get arrested and see Him get killed. All that makes Judas different is that he acts on his disappointment first, and worst.

And so in this sense, what Judas did is pretty ordinary. When Jesus wasn't who he wanted Him to be, he saved his skin. He got out while the going was good. We'll come back to this; but first we need to look at another friend of Jesus— one who had sworn never to let Him down.

Peter: The *Even Worse* Friend

It's hard to imagine a worse friend than Judas, but almost immediately that we've handed him the title, Peter throws his hat into the ring.

After Judas betrays Jesus, the crowd takes Him away to be interrogated at the home of the high priest. And outside the priest's home, the servants and hangers-on build a fire in the courtyard, doubtless talking about Jesus and His arrest. Peter, hoping not to be noticed, sits down and tries to be inconspicuous.

What happens next is well-known, simple and tragic. Peter denies that he knows Jesus three times. Luke tells the story quickly, but it's still excruciating. First, a slave girl says: "Hey, this guy was with Jesus!" Peter denies it. Then some random guy says: "Hey, you were with him". Peter denies it again. Then another person says: "You're from Galilee, you must be one of Jesus' disciples". Peter tells him that he doesn't even know what he's talking about.

For all his bluster about how he would die for Jesus, how he would never betray Him or deny Him (Luke 22 v 33), Peter totally crumples in the face of a question from a slave girl. No offense to any servant girls who might be reading this book, but this is pretty lame. Here's a guy who talked big talk about sticking with Jesus through thick and thin, and then a young girl asks a simple question and he folds.

And it isn't even that he lost his bottle once! One denial could have been a momentary lapse in judgment. But this was three times, separated by over an hour. He has plenty of time to think about it. And he keeps denying.

Just then a rooster crows. And Jesus, who had earlier told Peter that "before the rooster crows today, you will deny three times that you know me" (22 v 34), looks over. And as He looks at Peter, Peter realizes what he has done, and "he went outside and wept bitterly". He weeps tears of shame at his weakness, and of grief over what's happening to Jesus.

The question is: what has happened to Peter? Why on earth would he deny Jesus three times? John's Gospel tells us that it was Peter who cut off the servant's ear in the garden, so within the course of a couple of hours, Peter has gone from swinging a sword into the crowd to cowering before total strangers around a fire.

Why? What happened to Peter?

It had finally sunk in for him: Jesus was really going to die. He really wasn't going to fight back. He really was going to be crucified, just as He'd said. He had really meant all that stuff about being arrested and killed. There would be no revolution, no earthly glory, no great victory. Peter loved Jesus, there can be no doubt about that. But you get a sense that around that fire, he was just profoundly disappointed. He wanted something more; this wasn't what he had signed up for. He saved his own skin.

Peter or Judas?

In Peter and Judas, you have two great case studies of people who fail and abandon Jesus. And what you see in both of them is that they aren't along for the tough times. When times get hard, you see why they are really following Jesus. And both of them have an unspoken expectation of Jesus that He doesn't fulfill.

I don't think we're very different from Judas and Peter. Lots of people say they want to follow Jesus. Chances are that if you're reading this book, you want to follow Jesus. But the reasons *why* you want to follow Jesus will only become clear in the hard times.

After all, it's easy to follow Jesus when things are good. Everyone likes God when life is going along as you had hoped. But when you're not getting the things that you want, will you still follow Him? When it looks as if following Him is going to bring you benefit, it's fine. But when it becomes obvious that it will cost you, what will you do?

In the end, it boils down to this: do we love God, or do we love the things that He does for us? It's worth asking ourselves:

- What happens to my relationship with God when He isn't giving me the relationship or the money or the things I think I need in order to be happy?

- Have I ever complained to God that I've got it a lot worse than people who aren't Christians?

- Have I ever looked at other Christians who aren't as mature and hard-working as I feel I am, and angrily wondered why I am experiencing troubles while they skate by?

If the answer's yes, then you've got something in common with me—and you've got something of Judas in you. You've got something of Peter in you. It's so easy to betray Jesus in the ordinary course of day-to-day life. If you choose to believe the lie that Jesus isn't enough, or if you believe that He isn't living up to your expectations, it's a subtle but real form of betrayal. It's so easy to make big promises to God on Sunday, only to see them crumble when you are with your co-workers on Monday morning, or meeting up with friends on Tuesday evening.

But the call to follow Jesus is a call to endure and even suffer for His sake. It's a call to deny what's easiest for you, and give up earthly comfort; a call to follow Him and trust the course that He sets even when it seems that it's not "working" (Luke 9 v 23-24).

The Difference

OK, so that's the story. You've got Judas, and you've got Peter. Two disciples who both betray Jesus. Yet one has gone down in history as the ultimate villain, while the other went on to become a hero. Why?

What made the difference is what they did next. Matthew's Gospel tells us the next and final part of Judas' life:

> When Judas, who had betrayed him, saw that Jesus was condemned, he was seized with remorse and returned the thirty silver coins to the chief priests and the elders. "I have sinned," he said, "for I have betrayed innocent blood." "What is that to us?" they replied. "That's your responsibility." So Judas threw the money into the temple and left. Then he went away and hanged himself.
>
> (Matthew 27 v 3-5)

Too late, Judas changed his mind. He may well have shed tears, just like Peter. Certainly he felt great guilt. He regretted what he had done and the consequences that it brought.

Judas felt badly... but that was it. We never see him ask for forgiveness or turn to live for God. He just felt remorse. In 2 Corinthians 7 v 10, Paul writes: "Godly sorrow brings repentance that leads to salvation and leaves no regret, but worldly sorrow brings death". Judas is an example of this worldly sorrow. He felt regret; and it sent him to his death.

Peter, on the other hand, repented. He wept bitter tears for his sins, but he didn't just weep. You can tell that he repented for his sins because his life changed after that moment. He became bold and courageous for Christ. After the crucifixion, he joined with the other disciples for prayer. He was the first disciple to enter the empty tomb. After Jesus' resurrection from the dead, Peter was reconciled to Him and received forgiveness from Him, just as Jesus had predicted (Luke 22 v 32).

And so later on in his life, Peter could testify to the way that Jesus' death had secured forgiveness for people far from

God: "For Christ died for sins once for all, the righteous for the unrighteous, to bring you to God" (1 Peter 3 v 18).

Judas and Peter's guilt were the same: their responses were very different. When you stumble—whether it's an obvious moral failure you can't hope to hide, or a subtle pattern of pride that you don't want to admit to—how do you respond?

Judas and Peter show us there are four options:

- First, like the religious leaders, you can focus all your energies on the things you don't like about other people. Instead of dealing with their own issues, they obsessed over getting Jesus.

- You can try to make up for your mistakes, like Judas giving back the money he had received. The problem is, of course, that you can't un-ring a bell and you can't undo your sins.

- You can give in to despair, stew in your guilt and let it eat you alive, as Judas did.

- Or you can repent, as Peter did. You can bring your sin before God for mercy and put things in place that will help you change the way you live.

Only the last of these paths leads to life. And it only leads to life because of the One who loved the betrayer even as he betrayed Him; who looked at the denier even as he denied Him; and then went to the cross to die the death of a guilty man. Jesus died to pay the price for the sins of anyone who would come to Him in true repentance and faith.

Jesus: The Best Friend Ever!

We've already seen Jesus' love for Judas. He loved Him even as He faced His own arrest. And Jesus loved Peter, too. There in the middle of His trial, Jesus hears the rooster crow and His thoughts are all for Peter. When the rooster crowed, "the Lord turned and looked straight at Peter" (Luke 22 v 61).

If I had a friend that I had warned over and over again that he was going to fail me in my hour of need, and if that friend talked all kinds of trash about how great he was and how he'd do anything for me, and if that friend then failed me colossally, just as I'd predicted, I would have given him a look as well. I would have glared at him with an expression that was attempting to communicate: "I told you so, you disloyal moron!"

But that wasn't what Peter needed. He needed forgiveness. If Peter was going to move forward and not die in his guilt and shame like Judas, he needed a new start. His guilt was clear. It was not a question of whether he'd done something wrong. It was a question of how he could possibly go on from there.

When we're honest about ourselves, we know that this is what we need today. We're all guilty of trying to use God for our own ends. We obey Him when we want something from Him. When we don't like what He wants us to do, or when He doesn't do what we'd like Him to do, we go our own way. The question isn't whether we're guilty; it's *how we deal with that guilt.* Do we seek to shift it; seek to work it off; carry it till it crushes us; or give it to Jesus, let Him deal with it, and know the burden-lifting wonder of a clean slate?

If you are reading this book and you are not presently following Christ, what you need most is a new start. You need help with your guilt. You need Jesus.

And if you are following Christ? You need Jesus, too. His love for you—rather than your past achievements or service of Him—is what assures you that you are right with God.

Do you realize that as Jesus died, He took Peter's sin upon Himself? One of His closest friends denied even knowing Him in order to save his own skin, but Jesus responded by giving up His life in order to save His cowardly friend.

That ought to encourage you greatly. Jesus loves you as much as He loved Peter.

If you find yourself ensnared in some kind of sin, if you someday find yourself guilty of cowardice or betrayal, if you fail Jesus (and don't we all?), take fresh joy in the fact that Jesus knew your every weakness, your every failure, your every sin. He knew the worst about you. *And He died for you anyway.* Not so that He could hold you at arm's length for the rest of your life and hold over your head the things you've done, but so that you might be free, forgiven, and fully restored. All at a most awful cost to Himself.

He is a friend who will never betray you. He is a friend who will never abandon you. He is a friend who takes your guilt and deals with it and makes it so that in God's sight you never did it. That's the kind of friend you and I need. And in Jesus, that is the kind of friend we have.

For Reflection:

- *As you look at your last month, how have you been like Judas and Peter in ordinary, everyday ways?*

- *What one thing, if it were taken away, would be most likely to make you stop loving God?*

- *Other than asking Jesus to die for it, which of the three methods of dealing with guilt do you most often find yourself using?*

Jesus! What a friend for sinners!
Jesus! Lover of my soul;
Friends may fail me, foes assail me,
He, my Savior, makes me whole.

Jesus! What a strength in weakness!
Let me hide myself in Him;
Tempted, tried, and sometimes failing,
He, my strength, my vict'ry wins.

Jesus! I do now receive Him,
More than all in Him I find,
He hath granted me forgiveness,
I am His, and He is mine.

"Jesus! What a Friend for Sinners" by J. Wilbur Chapman

CHAPTER THREE

THE MOCKERY

⁶³ The men who were guarding Jesus began mocking and beating him. ⁶⁴ They blindfolded him and demanded, "Prophesy! Who hit you?" ⁶⁵ And they said many other insulting things to him.

⁶⁶ At daybreak the council of the elders of the people, both the chief priests and teachers of the law, met together, and Jesus was led before them. ⁶⁷ "If you are the Christ," they said, "tell us."

Jesus answered, "If I tell you, you will not believe me, ⁶⁸ and if I asked you, you would not answer. ⁶⁹ But from now on, the Son of Man will be seated at the right hand of the mighty God."

⁷⁰ They all asked, "Are you then the Son of God?"

He replied, "You are right in saying I am."

⁷¹ Then they said, "Why do we need any more testimony? We have heard it from his own lips."

Luke 22 v 63-71

As a parent with five young children, I try to protect my kids from some of the harsh realities of the world around them. More than once my wife or I have scrambled to grab the remote control and turn off the news because one of the kids has wandered into the room just as the newsreader started describing some gruesome accident or vicious crime from the previous day. It seems to me that there are some things little ones shouldn't have to know about.

But for all of our efforts, I can see them starting to put the pieces together. Ours is a pastor's home, so a lot of broken and needy people wind up at our dinner table at one time or another. And so my children have learned more about homelessness, teen pregnancy, gangs, and broken relationships than I might have ideally wanted to teach them at their tender ages.

On some level, I'm OK with that. But the one thing from which I am most trying to protect them is the flat-out cruelty of which human beings are capable. Face it; people can be horrible to each other. From the petty viciousness of school-age bullies to the massive atrocities that nation states and ethnic groups inflict on each other, the world we live in is pockmarked by acts of senseless cruelty. How do you explain that to a child? How do you help prepare them to live in a world where people sometimes fly airplanes into buildings occupied by total strangers? In a way, you can't explain it. It doesn't make any sense.

You don't have to be part of a church for long to begin to understand why Jesus died on the cross—to take the cup of God's wrath on behalf of sinful people. But, just as we see happening in our world today, in His final hours Jesus had to endure several rounds of senseless cruelty at the hands of His captors. Why? He was headed to the cross—why did He have to go through all of this extra abuse as well?

Jesus on Trial

Now that they have arrested Jesus, the religious leaders have a problem. Jewish law required that any charge which carried a death sentence be heard by an official meeting of the Sanhedrin, a group of 71 men including respected leaders, teachers of the religious law, and prominent priests (Luke usually refers to this group as "the assembly" or "the council"). Such a meeting had to take place during daylight hours; you can understand why the law would forbid trials and judgments carried on under the cover of darkness.

But Jesus is arrested late in the evening. And the leaders can't afford to sit on Him for very long. Jesus has many supporters in the city, and religious fervor is already high due to the Passover season, so the leaders don't dare wait and let the word get out that He has been arrested. They want to get things wrapped up, and have Him condemned and put to death as soon as possible.

But there is some delay before they can get the trial started, and under the cover of night and with some time on their hands, the guards who are watching Jesus begin to have a little fun with Him. They beat Jesus, mock Him, hurl insults at Him as they strike Him (the Greek word that Luke uses indicates that the beating went on for a prolonged period). Jesus has a reputation as a prophet, so they decide to put His skills to the test. They blindfold Him and punch Him, tauntingly challenging Him to guess who it was who hit Him.

Can you even begin to feel what it is like to be blindfolded, to be punched, to lose track of time as you wonder where the next bout of intense pain is coming from? It's easy to become familiar with these events so that they lose their sting, but the cruelty that's on display here is really stomach churning. How can people be this horrible to another human being? Jesus had never done anything to any one of them. But still they beat Him. Luke's account spares us all the details, simply telling us: "they said many other insulting things to him" (22 v 65), but you can imagine the vile insults and cruel taunts they hurled at Him.

This is a story of gratuitous cruelty and fiendish delight at the suffering of an innocent man. And *this* innocent man was God the Son. So why does Jesus have to suffer this indignity before His crucifixion? Isn't it bad enough that He will die a horrible death? Does He have to be subjected to this sickening treatment? Jesus will die to bear the penalty for the sins of His people. But He's not paying that price here as He is spat upon and smacked and taunted. So why?!

It's easier to answer that question if you remember who is in control here. We must be totally clear that Jesus could stop all of this torture if He wanted to. In Matthew's account of Jesus' arrest, He tells His disciples not to resist the men who have come to take Him into custody, saying:

> Do you think that I cannot call on my Father, and he will at once put at my disposal more than twelve legions of angels? But how then would the Scriptures be fulfilled that say it must happen in this way? (Matthew 26 v 53-54)

Jesus could stop this mocking if He wanted to, but He doesn't. The events of the next 24 hours must fulfill the Scriptures. Jesus is aware that His final hours have already been laid out centuries before by God's prophets.

Isaiah, looking forward over seven centuries, says of Him: "There were many who were appalled at him—his appearance was so disfigured beyond that of any man and his form marred beyond human likeness" (52 v 14). Jesus knew for His whole life that He would be beaten to the point where He no longer looked like a human being. Isaiah 50 v 6 puts these words in the mouth of the servant of the LORD: "I offered my back to those who beat me, my cheeks to those who pulled out my beard; I did not hide my face from mocking and spitting". The Christ would willingly subject Himself to all kinds of humiliation and scorn.

So Jesus had to endure this ordeal in order to fulfill prophecy. But that's a bit of a circular answer. Jesus had to endure this to fulfill prophecy... but why did it have to be prophesied?

The text doesn't tell us. But think of it this way: what does it mean for us that our Savior—the Son of God, the One who we worship and pray to—has experienced this kind of abuse? What does it mean that He knew this kind of undeserved malice from other men?

He Understands

It means that in all of your life, no matter what happens, you'll never experience any kind of suffering that Jesus didn't experience. He may not have endured the exact same abuse that you have encountered, but He knows fully what it means to be brutally mistreated by people. You can't go through anything that Jesus looks at and says: "I don't know what that's like".

That is a great comfort to us. We can "consider him who endured such opposition from sinful men, so that you will not grow weary and lose heart" (Hebrews 12 v 3).

When other people are unkind to us, when they abuse us (in small ways or in big ways), when we are mocked or shut out because we love Jesus, it can make us weary. It can tempt us to give up and wonder if God really cares. If that's where you are right now, take comfort in the fact that you can go to Jesus and find a loving and empathetic refuge in your time of distress. You won't find Him distant or unconcerned, but able to sympathize with all of your weakness and pain. We don't always know why God allows our suffering, but we do know that we never have to walk through it alone.

The suffering of Jesus also helps us in those times in life when we're called upon to comfort others who have been hurt. As a pastor, I talk to a lot of teenagers who have experienced terrible trauma and injustice in their short lives. And the one question that almost all of them ask is:

"If God is there, why did He let this happen to me?" Maybe you've been asked that question; maybe you've asked that question yourself.

Ultimately, we don't have a specific answer to that question. We simply don't know why God allows the individual events in our lives—good as well as bad—to happen. His purposes are simply too far above us for us to grasp.

But what we're really asking in those times of trouble is: "Is God good? Does He love me? Does He care? Does this matter to Him?" And Jesus' suffering at the hands of soldiers is, in a sense, God's answer to those heart-felt questions. God cares so much and He loves us so much that He sent His Son to endure this kind of hostility from sinners. He knows. He understands. He's been through it. God was *here*, and He let it happen to *Him*.

Sometimes that is our only answer, and it is enough. It is enough to make all the difference, both in this life and in the life to come. In fact, it doesn't only comfort me in my suffering; it transforms my response to my suffering. It means we are able not only to endure hardship, but actually glorify God in the midst of it.

Look at the apostle Peter's reflection on the way Jesus was treated by these mocking men:

> If you suffer for doing good and you endure it, this is commendable before God. To this you were called, because Christ suffered for you, leaving you an example, that you should follow in his steps. "He committed no sin, and no deceit was found in his mouth." When they hurled their insults at him, he did not retaliate; when he suffered, he made no threats. Instead, he entrusted himself to him who judges justly. (1 Peter 2 v 20-23)

Christians have not only the promise of the presence of Christ in our times of trial, we also have the pattern of Christ to guide us. When we suffer, we don't have to wonder how we can honor God. Peter tells us five things about Jesus' conduct when He suffered the pain and indignity of His last hours:

- He did not sin.
- He did not lie (presumably to get out of the situation).
- He did not insult His persecutors.
- He did not threaten them.
- He trusted His Father to judge all things justly.

Obviously, Jesus' experience is in many ways unique. You and I will never be called upon to suffer for other people's sins. But nonetheless we can "follow in his steps". When we are wronged, we should resist the temptation to take matters into our own hands. Instead of lying, threatening and insulting in order to get the results that we want, we ought to trust that God sees all, knows all, and will bring everything to justice in His own timing. We can accept that there are limits to the justice that we can know here and now. Ultimately, things will not be right until Jesus returns and judges the world.

God is Not Just a Victim

But we shouldn't think that Jesus' sufferings somehow mean that He was standing there as an impotent weakling. Some people have looked at Jesus' sufferings and concluded that He must have come to be a victim, that His greatest contribution to humanity was to show us how inhumanely we often treat each other. But thank God, literally, that's not the whole story, because we don't need a victim; we need a Savior. A weak God, a God who stands by wringing His hands idly while we decide what to do with Him and each other, is no God at all.

If Jesus is only a suffering innocent, His story may move us, but it cannot help us. But Jesus is much, much more than a victim of a show trial, as He points out to His accusers while being tried for His life.

The priests and elders and teachers thought they were the big shots, the powerful ones in the room. As they gather together to cross-examine the son of a carpenter from a two-bit backwoods town, they make a terrifying group. Here is the very highest court in the land, meeting to interrogate (and intimidate) Jesus of Nazareth. So in Luke 22 v 67, they put the question to Him directly: if He thinks He is the Christ (the Messiah, God's anointed King), they want Him to say so. They have already made their minds up about the answer; but they're hoping He'll incriminate Himself. They want to condemn Jesus quickly, not search for truth carefully.

Jesus knows as much, and calls them out for speaking out of the sides of their mouths. "If I tell you, you will not believe me" (v 67). It's a courtroom which places a very low value on truth.

But even so, as Jesus stands before this religious court, looking for all the world like a helpless victim, He points past that moment in time to the day when things would be quite different. "The Son of Man will be seated at the right hand of the mighty God" (v 69). He condemns Himself in order to challenge their understanding, and ours, of what is going on.

The "Son of Man" is a mysterious figure in Daniel 7 v 13-14, where the prophet says:

> In my vision at night I looked, and there before me was one like a son of man, coming with the clouds of heaven. He approached the Ancient of Days and was led into his presence. He was given authority, glory and sovereign power; all peoples, nations and men of every language worshiped him. His dominion is an everlasting dominion that will not pass away, and his kingdom is one that will never be destroyed.

That is a breathtaking scene! And it means that Jesus' claim is no less breathtaking. He is the all-powerful King, who receives authority from the eternal God, the Ancient of Days, to rule over the universe. He might be suffering as He stands before His accusers, but He will one day return in power and majesty. He might be the judged now, but there will be a day when He is the Judge. This is not just a suffering man; this is the ruling Son of Man.

Tragically, His accusers don't pause to consider the implications of the truth that the One they are about to murder is the One who will decide their eternal future. They are looking for self-incrimination; here they have it, spectacularly. If there were any doubts that they would not allow Him to continue drawing breath, they are gone at this point.

Jesus the Judge

There is a great irony in the fact that Jesus is standing trial before the religious leaders of the people. Step back for a second and recognize how crazy this is: the religious leaders have put God on trial. They are going to sit in judgment over Him! And what's even more insane is that they find Him guilty! Not only that, but they actually find him guilty of blasphemy, of lying about God! This is like a group of nine-year-olds in an art class finding Michelangelo guilty of crimes against art, and of producing fake copies of Michelangelo paintings... only infinitely worse.

Now, when people in the Bible have a close encounter with the majesty of God, they have one response: terror. They fall down on their faces (Revelation 1 v 17); they scream (Isaiah 6 v 5); they hide themselves (Exodus 3 v 6). Earlier in Luke's Gospel, when one of God's angels appeared to a group of shepherds, they were "terrified" (Luke 2 v 9). So when Jesus reveals His identity to the men who are sitting in judgment over Him, they should bow before Him. If nothing else, they should experience a moment of overwhelming and abject terror as they realize they have just been party to punching the God of the universe in the face. But their hearts are hard; they have already decided that Jesus must die.

Can you see how horrific this scene is? It's like one of those bad dreams where everything is the exact opposite of the way it should be. It's a miscarriage of justice for the ages. But it's also a perfect picture of the humility and love of God. The Almighty Creator allows His creatures to treat Him like this.

And in a sense, God condescends to allow each and every one of us to pass judgment on Him. God calls us to decide what we will make of His Son Jesus—to decide whether He is worthy of our exclusive love and worship and devotion as He claimed, or whether He is a blasphemer and a liar as His enemies believed.

Every person who hears the message about Jesus must put themselves in the place of the religious leaders, and decide who they believe Him to be.

If you are reading this book and you are not a follower of Christ, then, to put it bluntly, you are casting your vote along with the chief priests and teachers of the law. Perhaps you're doing it in a polite and well-mannered way, but that's the way your vote goes.

Don't be deceived by God's kindness. Jesus stands before these men absorbing their scorn and abuse, but He also promises to return, not to suffer but to bring judgment to all those who have rejected Him. Mark records Jesus' full reply at His trial as: "You will see the Son of Man sitting at the right hand of the Mighty One *and coming on the clouds of heaven*" (Mark 14 v 62). Right now, we all have the life and breath to decide whether we will willingly worship God's Son or not. But one day, everyone will bow their knee to King Jesus (Philippians 2 v 9-11). The only question is whether each of us will do so in joyful welcome or in quaking terror.

On that day, wrongs will be set right, senseless cruelty will be dealt with, and the suffering that pockmarks our world will cease. Until then, you and I will suffer. I'll still have people eating at our family table who have been pushed to rock bottom through no fault of their own.

What will I say to them? What will we say to ourselves? That as sons and daughters of our Father in heaven (Matthew 5 v 45), we are free and strengthened to love those who persecute us, just as the Lord Jesus did. That while He suffered alone, we never have to, because we can go to Him with our cares and our tears and find compassion and understanding. That because we know that He is not ultimately a weak and powerless God, but a ruling, judging One, we can leave justice up to Him and get on with living and loving like Him.

Like any parent, I want to shield my kids from pain. If I had my way, they would never experience the cruelty of others or the sufferings that come from living in a broken world. But I know that that's impossible. Sooner or later, and far sooner than I'd like, they'll be exposed to pain and heartbreak and disappointment. So while it's good for me to protect them, it's even more important for them to understand that God loves them. And that's true for all of us as well. We might not know why God allows certain situations in our lives; we might not understand why he allows such cruelty in the world; but we know that He cares, that He loves us, and that He will one day make everything right.

And sometimes, that has to be enough.

For Reflection:

- *How much does the suffering of Jesus affect your attitude to your own suffering?*
- *What are the times in your life when you most need to remember that God understands?*
- *When are you most tempted to take justice into your own hands? How will knowing that Jesus is the Son of Man allow you to live the way that pleases Him, not the way that vindicates you?*

I cannot tell how silently He suffered,
As with His peace He graced this place of tears.
Or how His heart upon the cross was broken,
The crown of pain to three and thirty years.
But this I know, He heals the broken-hearted,
And stays our sin, and calms our lurking fear,
And lifts the burden from the heavy laden,
For yet the Savior, Savior of the world, is here.

I cannot tell how He will win the nations,
How He will claim His earthly heritage,
How satisfy the needs and aspirations
Of east and west, of sinner and of sage.
But this I know, all flesh shall see His glory,
And He shall reap the harvest He has sown,
And some glad day His sun shall shine in splendor
When He the Savior, Savior of the world, is known.

I cannot tell how all the lands shall worship,
When, at His bidding, every storm is stilled,
Or who can say how great the jubilation
When all the hearts of men with love are filled.
But this I know, the skies will thrill with rapture,
And myriad, myriad human voices sing,
And earth to heaven, and heaven to earth, will answer:
At last the Savior, Savior of the world, is King.

"I Cannot Tell" by William Young Fullerton

CHAPTER FOUR

THREE KINGS

¹ Then the whole assembly rose and led him off to Pilate. ² And they began to accuse him, saying, "We have found this man subverting our nation. He opposes payment of taxes to Caesar and claims to be Christ, a king."

³ So Pilate asked Jesus, "Are you the king of the Jews?" "Yes, it is as you say," Jesus replied.

⁴ Then Pilate announced to the chief priests and the crowd, "I find no basis for a charge against this man."

⁵ But they insisted, "He stirs up the people all over Judea by his teaching. He started in Galilee and has come all the way here."

⁶ On hearing this, Pilate asked if the man was a Galilean. ⁷ When he learned that Jesus was under Herod's jurisdiction, he sent him to Herod, who was also in Jerusalem at that time.

⁸ When Herod saw Jesus, he was greatly pleased, because for a long time he had been wanting to see him. From what he had heard about him, he hoped to see him perform some miracle. ⁹ He plied him with many questions, but Jesus gave him no answer.
¹⁰ The chief priests and the teachers of the law were standing there, vehemently accusing him. ¹¹ Then Herod and his soldiers ridiculed and mocked him. Dressing him in an elegant robe, they sent him back to Pilate. ¹² That day Herod and Pilate became friends—before this they had been enemies.   Luke 23 v 1-12

Monarchy really isn't in vogue these days. As an American, I have no sense of what it would be like to be under the rule of a king or queen. Even in places like Great Britain where there is a monarchy, and where the monarch is much-loved by many, the royal family's role is largely symbolic. There aren't many people clamoring for the good old days of a single, absolute, divine-right ruler.

After all, history has repeatedly shown that the fatal flaw of monarchy is... the monarchs. Simply being born into a particular family doesn't mean you're well qualified to exercise authority over a nation or empire. History is littered with hereditary rulers who were awful at ruling. Take Ferdinand I of Austria, for example. The result of some serious inbreeding, Ferdinand was described by a contemporary as having "an over-large head with a flat skull". Apparently he loved to amuse himself by wedging himself in a wastepaper basket and rolling over and over like a ball. Not exactly the kind of guy you'd want to hold the power of life and death over you. Nor King Alonso VI of Portugal, aka "Alonso the Glutton". Or Charles VI of France, otherwise known as "Charles the Mad".

The list goes on, but you get the point. Royalty doesn't work all that well because for the most part the royals aren't very good at running the world.

But what if there were a perfect king? What if there were someone who was perfectly wise, perfectly just, perfectly selfless and perfectly loving? Who always knew what the right thing to do was, and always did it? Wouldn't you want that person to make all the decisions, rather than democratically stepping aside and letting us pool our best guesses and muddle through?

If you could have a king like that, wouldn't it be great to live in a monarchy?

Luke wants to point us to such a ruler. And He's neither the all-powerful Roman governor, nor the reigning Jewish king, who we meet in this scene.

Two Terrible Rulers

It helps to know the back story of the two rulers Luke introduces us to at the start of chapter 23.

Pontius Pilate was a Roman prefect. His job was to rule over the region of Judea for the Roman emperor. As long as he collected the taxes and prevented uprisings, the authorities in Rome didn't care what he did to the people of Israel. And by all accounts Pilate was a ruthless ruler. History tells us that he was known in his day for executing criminals without a trial, stealing money from the Jewish temple, and intentionally offending the people of Jerusalem by putting up statues of the Roman emperor, or "Caesar", around the city.

Herod Antipas was the king of Galilee, the area north of Jerusalem itself. He was a puppet ruler, exercising authority only with Rome's blessing. And like Pontius Pilate, Antipas was not a good man. At one point, he married his brother's wife and threw the prophet John the Baptist in jail for objecting to the marriage. At his birthday party some time later, Antipas got drunk, ogled his niece (who was now also his step-daughter), and had John beheaded at her mother's request (Matthew 14 v 6-11). This is not a guy you'd want to have over to watch the football on the weekend.

It is before these two men that Jesus will now stand trial. The Sanhedrin have condemned Jesus to death. But they're not allowed to execute prisoners. Rome had long since revoked their right to inflict capital punishment. So the members of the Sanhedrin need to convince Pilate to do the actual execution.

That presents them with a big problem: Jesus hasn't done anything that would make the Roman authorities want to execute Him! Pilate doesn't care at all about the ways that Jesus has offended their religious customs. He won't execute Jesus just because the Jewish leaders think He is a blasphemer. So in verse 2, the Sanhedrin lodges three charges against Jesus that might serve to get Pilate's interest.

First, they claim that He has been "subverting our nation". The idea is that Jesus is dangerous, and might start a mob rebellion against Roman rule.

Second, they claim that Jesus "opposes payment of taxes to Caesar". This would be guaranteed to get Pilate's attention. The only downside is that it is the exact opposite of what Jesus had really taught (see Luke 20 v 20-26).

The third charge, though, is the best. It is actually true, and it is explosive: Jesus "claims to be Christ". In case Pilate doesn't appreciate what the Christ (or Messiah) means, they translate it into naked political language. It means He claims to be "a king".

And it's that last charge that gets Pilate's attention. He questions Jesus directly: "Are you the king of the Jews?" (v 3). There's a bit of mockery in the way Pilate asks the question. In the original Greek it reads: "You're the king of the Jews?" Jesus is standing there having been bound, blindfolded, and beaten. He's sleep-deprived and spit-covered. At this moment, He doesn't look particularly regal. And so Pilate seems a little amused and a little surprised. *You're* the king of the Jews? *You?!*

Jesus gives a somewhat cryptic answer to Pilate's question; it's basically the same answer that He gave to the Sanhedrin back in 22 v 70. He doesn't answer in the affirmative, but simply deflects by saying: "You have said so". It's an answer which doesn't really move things forward! You can imagine

Pilate thinking: "I know I have said that; I was here when I said it and I heard myself saying it!".

But what seems like a non-answer is, in fact, the only answer that makes sense.

Jesus is not a King

On one hand, Jesus can't deny that He is a king. He's just confirmed He will rule at God the Father's right hand, as the all-powerful Son of Man (22 v 69). But He also knows that He's not a king in the way that Pilate intends the question. Jesus simply is not what we think of when we think of a king. Kings aren't born in animal shelters, as Jesus was. They dress in gold instead of building with wood. They sleep in palaces, rather than having nowhere at all to lay their heads. They have influential, powerful followers, rather than a ragtag bag of fishermen, fighters and rejects. They don't stand quietly and passively, beaten, bloodied and bowed, in front of their people's enemy.

Jesus does not look like a king; and He doesn't have the ambitions of a king. Back in John 6, just after Jesus had miraculously fed 5,000 people, He realized that "they intended to come and make him king by force" (John 6 v 15). Here was a great chance to grab political power: but instead He "withdrew again to a mountain by himself". He was not the king they were looking for.

Yet people seemed to make this mistake about Jesus all the time; even John the Baptist got hot under the collar once or twice about it (see Luke 7 v 18-23). People would see that Jesus was obviously a special, powerful, influential leader, and when He started talking about bringing a kingdom, they would assume that He was going to make a run at political power. After all, this was what the Jewish people wanted and expected their Messiah to do. They longed for a king who would come and overthrow Rome and reestablish the glory of Israel. And who could blame them?

But then Jesus kept saying strange things like: "my kingdom is not of this world" (John 18 v 36); "[I] must suffer many things and be rejected … and … must be killed" (Luke 9 v 22) and "There are those who are last who will be first, and first who will be last" (Luke 13 v 30). He repeatedly made clear that He didn't want to be a ruler in the sense Herod and Pilate were rulers. If you were paying attention, you would have known perfectly well that Jesus wasn't aiming to lead an overthrow of Rome and establish His own earthly rule at the point of a sword. But sometimes people prefer not to pay attention, so that they can keep believing what they want to believe. They wanted a powerful political figure, a king who would war and win against their enemies, a ruler who would cut out the corruption from the Jewish elites. So that's who they chose to see.

Pilate and Herod, on the other hand, seemed to recognize the truth about Jesus immediately. These were two very paranoid men. Being a ruler in first-century Palestine was not a career path with a lot of job stability or a long-term growth trajectory. If you made the emperor mad, you were exiled (or worse). If your enemies got the jump on you, you were exiled (or worse). If some upstart started a popular revolution, you were finished. And so, unsurprisingly, both Pilate and Herod had a long track record of killing anyone who even hinted that they could be a threat.

But when they meet Jesus, who "claims to be Christ, a king", they do… nothing. Pilate sends Him to Herod; Herod just sends Him back. Jesus obviously poses absolutely no threat to anyone's political power. He is not a king like them; He's not after their positions.

Christians and Governments

This is a helpful reminder for those of us who are followers of Jesus twenty centuries later. Being His disciples will have implications for the way we relate to the authorities over us in the government. As Christians, we should obey the government, pray for our leaders, pay our taxes, and be grateful for the ways in which our state helps establish order and justice (1 Peter 2 v 13-17; Romans 13 v 1-7; 1 Timothy 2 v 1-2). We can and should be involved in government. It's perfectly appropriate for Christians to seek elected office and to shape the policies of their nation. In that sense, Christians should view government as a good thing.

But we mustn't be surprised when societies which are generally in rebellion against God's word have governments that pass laws opposed to the will of God. And so Christians should oppose laws that allow unjust practices (like abortion) and should speak clearly about issues that God's word addresses clearly (like same-sex marriage). In fact, Christians through history have been instrumental in banning inhumane practices, such as infanticide in ancient Rome (and modern China), slavery in North America and Britain, and suttee in India.

There is a sense of ambivalence in Scripture about human governments. Pretty much every one of the political rulers mentioned in the New Testament is questionable at best. The book of Revelation views the governments of the earth as opposed to God and putting His people to death (eg: Revelation 19 v 19). We are never encouraged to think that political systems will be a very fruitful avenue for spreading the gospel, or that they will supply the ultimate answer to our world's problems.

Jesus certainly didn't. The kingdom that Jesus came to establish was not an earthly, political entity. He was not primarily interested in policy decisions and matters of state. And so in the book of Acts, when Peter and John and Paul stand in front of corrupt and wicked rulers, they don't talk politics, they preach the gospel (4 v 1-20; 25 v 23 – 26 v 31). Likewise, Christians need to be realistic about what government can and cannot accomplish. Jesus' kingdom and Christian ethics are not ultimately going to be established by any political party.

Jesus *is* a King

Pilate knows a threat when he sees one. And he knows Jesus is no threat to him. So he concludes that "I find no basis for a charge against this man" (v 4). But of course the leaders of the Sanhedrin have come too far to give up now. They complain that Jesus has been stirring up trouble throughout Galilee (v 5); and suddenly Pilate sees a way out of this situation.

Roman law stated that a man could be tried for a crime either in the place where the alleged crime had occurred, or in his home province. So Pilate sends Jesus to Herod Antipas, trying to pass the buck to someone else. Herod, a man who seems to have liked to focus on his own importance in Galilee rather than his puppet status in Rome, perceives Pilate's actions as a courtesy and the two men become friends as they connive in this miscarriage of justice.

Herod is excited to see Jesus. He had loved to listen to John the Baptist (up until the point that he had him killed—ultimately, he loved sleeping with his brother's wife even more) and he has wanted to see Jesus for a long time (Luke 9 v 9). And so now he hopes to have Jesus come and do some tricks for him. But Jesus refuses, and so Herod and his men decide to have some fun with Him. "Dressing him in an elegant robe" that a king would wear (v 11), Herod's men ridicule Jesus, as if to say: "You wanna be a king? We'll make you a king!" They mock the idea that Jesus could be a king, just like Pilate's soldiers who crown His head with thorns (Matthew 27 v 27-31).

In all this, though they are unlikely to know it, Pilate and Herod are unwittingly fulfilling Psalm 2 v 2, written hundreds of years before:

> The kings of the earth take their stand and the rulers gather
> together against the LORD and against his Anointed One.

The man standing in front of them, if they would only pause to see, really is a king. Not a puppet king, or a temporary governor, but God's chosen Messiah, the Anointed One. These two rulers may not realize it, but Luke has prepared readers of his Gospel to understand that in this case, appearances really are deceptive. Jesus really is the long awaited king of the Jews (Luke 19 v 38 and 20 v 41-44), the descendant of the great King David (3 v 31), the "Son of the Most High" who would reign forever over a kingdom that would never end, as the angel Gabriel had told His mother Mary (1 v 31-33).

We're like the readers of a mystery who know more about the plot and characters than the people in the story themselves do. We can see the truth about Jesus, even if they can't. Jesus isn't a king like them; but He is a King. It turns out that Jesus is the real King in that room!

Yet this King's kingdom isn't coming through military might or political skill. His kingdom will be established on a cross, a brutal instrument of execution. As Pilate and Herod get on with their day, Jesus will be mocked as a common criminal, not eulogized as a glorious King.

But then He will rise from the dead in the greatest display of power in human history. His resurrection will be His public vindication, God the Father's verdict over-ruling the decision of the earthly courts and declaring His Son "not guilty". And after teaching His disciples and preparing them to spread His kingdom, Jesus will ascend to heaven to reign as King.

That's where He is right now, as you read this paragraph. Hebrews 2 v 9 tells us that by faith: "We see Jesus, who was made a little lower than the angels, now crowned with glory and honor because he suffered death". Because of His suffering, Jesus has received a royal crown and a heavenly throne.

And one day the King will return from heaven, rout all opposition, and consummate His eternal kingdom. That kingdom is described for us in Revelation 11 v 15:

> There were loud voices in heaven, which said, "The kingdom of the world has become the kingdom of our Lord and of his Christ, and he will reign for ever and ever."

We need to realize that the reason that Jesus was not after a political kingdom was *not* because it was too big a thing for Him, but because it was far too small. It's not that He couldn't have overthrown Rome and established a glorious kingdom in Israel. But that was small potatoes compared to Jesus' plans. The entire Roman empire, sweeping throughout the known world, couldn't contain the kingdom that He did want to establish. Jesus wasn't a king in the way that Pilate and Herod might mean the word: but He was (and is) a King. He is *the* King.

The King will Win

The implications of this are endless. Since Jesus is the now-enthroned, someday-returning King of the universe, He deserves, and rightly demands, that we should honor and obey Him as that King.

And since that glorious present-day King is also the man who suffered so much and seemed so defeated on that day in history, we need to see that we can't judge the Lord's final purpose by the way it appears at any given moment.

Jesus is always victorious, even when He seems to be losing. Standing before those two earthly rulers, Jesus was about as low as any human being can get: bloodied, beaten, abandoned, mocked, derided. Never had a claimant to kingship looked less like a ruler. But despite all of that suffering, Jesus is a king: the King of the Jews, and the King of everyone, everywhere, in every time and for all time.

There will be times in our lives as followers of Christ when it seems like His good purposes have been thwarted. Personal suffering can make Christ's ultimate victory look distant and unimaginable. Choices made by the people we love can make it appear that there is no way that things will ever end well for us. The evil of the world around us sometimes seems so overwhelming that God's plans appear defeated. Sometimes, if we're honest, the sin in our own lives is so discouraging that we feel as though Christ's purposes can never come to pass. But in all of those circumstances, Jesus is still the King of the universe, sovereign over every one of the details. Pilate and Herod were deceived by appearances. The Anointed One stood in front of them—and they failed to recognize Him. Let's not make the same mistake.

What situations in your life make you doubt Jesus' mighty rule? Where do you struggle to believe that God is in control? When are the times you need to remind yourself that if Jesus was in control before Pilate, if He was Messiah even while being taunted by Herod, then He is certainly in control over everything that happens in your life?

Actually, some of us don't so much doubt that Jesus the Messiah is great; rather, many Christians secretly (in the back of our minds, even if we wouldn't say it) doubt that He's good. Or, we believe that He is good in general, but He's not kindly disposed towards us individually. He doesn't want what's best for me; He's probably actually a little mad at me because of all the stuff I've done. Or He's simply too busy and too far away to be concerned with the details of my insignificant life. And so the suffering, the marriage problems, the family struggles, my children's futures, the job issues, the health problems, the depression, the loss... well, I just can't trust Jesus with it.

But when you see Jesus before Pilate and Herod, that all falls away. If God is too high and mighty to be concerned with you and your needs, how do you explain Jesus lowering Himself like this? If God doesn't care about you or if He isn't kind, then why did Jesus endure all of that? If you are a Christian, you're watching Him go to the cross for you! Do you think that he's going to turn on you now, after going through all of that? Do you think He died for you so that He can abandon you when you sin or stumble?

Monarchy is not much in fashion any more, but something deep in us wants a king. Think about the adventure stories that thrilled your soul as a child (or even today!). It's no coincidence that so many of them feature a king, a noble and wise and courageous and sacrificial ruler who delivers his people from their enemies. Those stories resonate with us because we were created to have exactly that kind of king. We were made to live under the authority of a perfect monarch; and the absolute rule of Jesus the Messiah will outlast all other political systems.

Herod and his men dressed Jesus in a royal robe as a mocking response to His claim to be a king. But when a

Christian thinks about Jesus in that robe, enduring the taunts and ridicule of the soldiers, we see the proof that Jesus is the heroic King we've always wanted. He is the One who is great and who is good. He alone is worthy of all our allegiance and trust, both in all the difficulties in all the details of our lives today, and as we face our eternal destiny. He's the King. And He's *our* King.

For Reflection:

- *How would your life change if you remembered that your friend Jesus is also the King of kings?*

- *Do you tend to make too much or too little of human political systems? How?*

- *How does the knowledge that Jesus is in charge of the details of your life encourage you today?*

Crown him with many crowns, the Lamb upon His throne.
Hark! How the heavenly anthem drowns all music but
its own.
Awake, my soul, and sing of Him who died for thee,
And hail Him as thy matchless King through all eternity.

Crown Him the Lord of heaven, enthroned in worlds above,
Crown Him the King to whom is given the wondrous name
of Love.
Crown Him with many crowns, as thrones before Him fall;
Crown Him, ye kings, with many crowns, for He is King
of all.

Crown Him the Lord of lords, who over all doth reign,
Who once on earth, the incarnate Word, for ransomed
sinners slain.
Now lives in realms of light, where saints with angels sing
Their songs before Him day and night, their God,
Redeemer, King.

Crown Him the Lord of years, the potentate of time,
Creator of the rolling spheres, ineffably sublime.
All hail, Redeemer, hail! For Thou hast died for me;
Thy praise and glory shall not fail throughout eternity.

"Crown Him with Many Crowns" by Matthew Bridges and Godfrey Thring

CHAPTER FIVE

AWAY WITH THIS MAN!

¹³ Pilate called together the chief priests, the rulers and the people, ¹⁴ and said to them, "You brought me this man as one who was inciting the people to rebellion. I have examined him in your presence and have found no basis for your charges against him. ¹⁵ Neither has Herod, for he sent him back to us; as you can see, he has done nothing to deserve death. ¹⁶ Therefore, I will punish him and then release him."

¹⁸ With one voice they cried out, "Away with this man! Release Barabbas to us!" (¹⁹ Barabbas had been thrown into prison for an insurrection in the city, and for murder.)

²⁰ Wanting to release Jesus, Pilate appealed to them again. ²¹ But they kept shouting, "Crucify him! Crucify him!"

²² For the third time he spoke to them: "Why? What crime has this man committed? I have found in him no grounds for the death penalty. Therefore I will have him punished and then release him."

²³ But with loud shouts they insistently demanded that he be crucified, and their shouts prevailed. ²⁴ So Pilate decided to grant their demand. ²⁵ He released the man who had been thrown into prison for insurrection and murder, the one they asked for, and surrendered Jesus to their will. Luke 23 v 13-25

As Jesus stands before Pilate, against the backdrop of the crowd of ordinary citizens and with the local religious and political leaders around Him, it's as though every kind of person is represented in that courtyard in Jerusalem. There is co-operation between Jews and Gentiles, the two groups of people that comprised the entire world for a first-century Palestinian. There are religious and political actors; this is the work of both church and state, so to speak. And there's the crowd, the great mass of unnamed people who turn the wheels of history in every age.

This universal scope invites us to locate ourselves within the story. We're drawn to put ourselves in the shoes of the different characters. We're challenged to ask ourselves: of all the people there that day, *who am I most like?* Who represents *me*?

And Luke's provocative answer is: all of them, except One.

You are Pontius Pilate

The key thing to remember about Pilate is that he is absolutely convinced that Jesus is innocent. In verse 14 he tells the Jewish leaders that his investigation has turned up no evidence against Jesus. He points out in verse 15 that Herod apparently came to the same conclusion. And so in verse 20 he wants to release Jesus, and in verse 22 he responds to the cries of the crowd: "Why? What crime has this man committed? I have found in him no grounds for the death penalty."

Pilate knows Jesus is innocent. But he won't simply free Him, because he doesn't want to anger the Jewish leaders who think He is guilty. So throughout this scene, he's repeatedly trying to avoid making a decision one way or the other. But in the end, he still hands Jesus over to be crucified. Pilate has the power to protect the innocent; instead, he sends Him to His death.

It's at this point that Matthew's Gospel includes the famous detail of Pilate washing his hands of the whole affair (Matthew 27 v 24). But just because you say you aren't responsible for a decision, and dip your hands in some water, doesn't mean that you really are innocent. By Luke 23 v 25, there is only one truly innocent man in the scene; and He's heading off to a cross.

It's easy to condemn Pilate, isn't it? His name has become synonymous with treachery, weakness, and corruption. Surely we could never do anything like that... could we? If the innocent Lord of creation had stood before us, we would never have sent Him to His death... would we?

But what is Pilate's crime, ultimately? Why did he do this notorious and unjust thing? Luke gives us a clue in verses 23-25. In verse 23, "their voices prevailed". Pilate "decided to grant their demand" (v 24), and so he "surrendered Jesus to their will" (v 25).

Pilate is forced to make a decision: will he do the right thing, or the popular thing? Will he fear God, or fear man? It's easy to criticize Pilate—and it's right to—but let's pause to ask ourselves: have we ever chosen to do what was easy rather than what was right? Have we ever done something that we knew was wrong because we knew it would please someone else? I need to ask myself: have I ever compromised on my convictions, or kept silent when I should have spoken, or just decided that it would be better to go along with the crowd?

If your answer to those questions is "no", then there are two options: you're as perfect as Jesus Christ, or you need to put this book down and go and get a book about self-awareness. But for the rest of us, those of us who answer "yes", at those moments we were in Pilate's shoes... and we did what Pilate did. Our actions were different from his in degree, but not in kind. Just like him, we were letting others control our behavior. We wanted to do what was popular more than we wanted to do what was right. So while we've probably never done anything as awful as what Pilate did, that's only because we've never had the opportunity.

The root of Pilate's crime is cowardice. He has already had a few blunders on his watch (including setting off a riot in Jerusalem by offending Jewish religious sensibilities) and he can't allow a negative report to get back to Caesar. So here, as Jesus stands before him, Pilate can't afford to alienate the Jewish religious leaders, who might be able to sink his career. He can't risk being accused of letting a rival ruler to Caesar go free. So he chooses to cave in, in one of the most spectacular ways possible.

Cowardice isn't always or often as spectacular as this. More often, it's subtle. And while it wreaks very real havoc in many different circumstances, it is particularly damaging when it lodges itself in the hearts of leaders. The fact that Pilate is in a position of leadership makes the consequences of his cowardice all the more terrible. Here he is, in a position of authority given to him by God for the purpose of punishing evil and protecting the innocent (Romans 13 v 1-4). But he uses his position to punish and destroy the innocent, all because he is afraid.

Those of us who are in leadership need to be on particular guard against cowardice in our hearts. It is so easy actively to do the wrong thing, or even easier passively not to do the right thing, simply in order to please other people. But the consequences can be felt over many generations.

For example, the Bible teaches that men are supposed to be leaders in their homes. But isn't it much easier to be passive, just doing whatever it takes to keep the peace? Isn't it easier not to lead or set the agenda in our homes, or offer loving direction to our families, because we are afraid that our wives will become angry or simply won't follow us? Isn't it so much more comfortable to do what our wives want, instead of even considering what they need? Or—let's face it—to do what we want, rather than what they need?

Staying in the home, parents are meant to lead their children, but often it's actually children who lead. Their comfort is primary, their opinions are central, and their desires shape family life. Why? Perhaps because deep down we're terrified that if we don't revolve everything around our kids, they'll hate us when they grow up, or they'll wind up on a psychiatrist's couch somewhere, complaining about how mom and dad never loved them. And so couples end up neglecting their own marriages and revolving everything around the kids' fencing lessons and violin classes and Mandarin tutoring.

Perhaps the easiest, and most tragic, place to witness cowardly leadership is in the church. When church leaders won't do or say unpopular things, the church withers and dies—or, worse, it becomes a social club that allows its members falsely to assume all is well between this world and its Maker. When church leaders make decisions driven by fear of man, the true church disappears. The truth is frequently unpopular, and standing up for God's word and against sin will sometimes make people angry. We need church leaders who aren't directed by popularity polls, but whose decision-making is dominated by what is right.

So let's examine our lives. Is there an area—in the home, in the workplace, in the church—where you should be leading, but you have been afraid? This isn't to encourage leadership that disregards the opinions of others, or which is arrogant or proud or insensitive. But leaders do need to be courageous. If everyone else were always right, the world wouldn't need leadership. If everyone else were always right, there would only be one political party! So whether you are a leader in your home or the workplace or in the church, check to see where you may be leading out of fear of other people.

But we're not only like Pilate in being cowardly leaders. We can also be like him by being cowards when it comes to suffering for Christ. That's another way of describing Pilate's sin. He approves of Jesus, he marvels at Him, he proclaims His innocence, but he's not willing to suffer for Him in any way. When Jesus becomes too inconvenient, Pilate is out.

So again, we need to see where in our lives we stand in his shoes. Have you ever been anything less than wholeheartedly committed to Christ because it would cost you in the eyes of other people? Have you ever laughed at a dirty joke or joined in some vicious gossip when you should have kept your mouth shut, so that you're part of the group? Have you ever engaged in sinful behavior so you wouldn't seem odd or strange?

Those questions sting me. I can't kid myself that I'm any better than Pilate. After all, he was facing an angry mob and possible exile by the emperor. I cave in at the thought of mild disapproval by people I don't even like that much. Perhaps you do, too.

Breaking the Power of Cowardice

It's hard to be honest enough to recognize our own cowardice. It's still harder to break its hold on our hearts. How can we do it?

First, we need to fear God more. Fearing God means worshipping Him, knowing His holiness, trusting in Him, relying on Him above all other people and things, and hoping in Him. Fearing the Lord is the knowledge both of God's holiness and His mercy, His wrath and His forgiveness. In Luke 12 v 4-5, Jesus puts it pretty bluntly:

> I tell you, my friends, do not be afraid of those who kill the body and after that can do no more. But I will show you whom you should fear: Fear him who, after the killing of the body, has the power to throw you into hell. Yes, I tell you, fear him.

For those who live shamelessly for Christ in this life, fearing God isn't about abject terror, because "the Son of Man will ... acknowledge him before the angels of God" (Luke 12 v 8). Fearing the Lord is about being more concerned with God's judgment than the judgment of our peers.

When we fear the Lord, we understand that God graciously initiates our relationship with Him and then we respond with love and worship. We develop the fear of the Lord by reading His word, knowing Him more fully, and being more aware of His gaze than the gaze of our friends, children, spouse, co-workers, and fellow church members. When we fear God, we act in ways we know will please God rather than ways designed to please other people.

To combat our natural cowardice, we need to fear God more—and, second, we also need to love people more. When we fear other people, we can't actually love them; we only want them for their approval. It's really quite selfish. We withhold from people the things that they need from us, because we fear that they might cut us off from the things that we want from them. We want their approval more than we want to do and say the things that are helpful for them, whether that's a tough leadership decision or telling them about Christ. Love has the power to displace cowardice.

But ultimately, believing the gospel is the key to solving our fear problem. If you grasp the magnitude of what God has done for you in Christ, then He will become the primary object of your love and affection. His gaze will be the most important in your life. When you understand that Christ's death secures your total acceptance and approval before God, then you won't be so concerned about what other people think about you.

And when you no longer need everyone else's approval, you can be free to love them truly and care for them selflessly.

You are the Crowd

Pilate comes out and proclaims Jesus' innocence, but Luke tells us that "with one voice they cried out" (v 18) for Jesus to be crucified. Who are the "they"? It's the chief priests, the rulers and the people—everyone else.

They all cry out together. This is a universal, unanimous verdict from people of every walk of life and social class. *Everyone* cries out: "Get rid of Him!" Five days previously, crowds had hailed Jesus as a king; now, crowds are calling for His blood.

In Acts 3 v 13-15, Peter places the blame squarely on the crowd. Speaking to the men of Israel, he says:

> The God of our fathers has glorified his servant Jesus. You handed him over to be killed, and you disowned him before Pilate, though he had decided to let him go. You disowned the Holy and Righteous One and asked that a murderer be released to you. You killed the author of life.

Why? Why do they call for His death so viciously? Surely there is some mob mentality there—people do crazy things when the crowd is going in that direction. Perhaps there is a sense of disappointment with Jesus. This guy obviously isn't the king who is going to overthrow Rome. He's a fake; he's a phony.

But perhaps there is something deeper going on, because in that shout we see most clearly the natural state of man. We are, at our core, God's enemies. There, in the howling hatred of the crowd, we see something of our natural attitude towards God. When it came down to a choice, they prefer to have a murderer live among them rather than God Himself.

Human beings simply can't be neutral towards God. There is no middle ground. He is perfectly holy. We were created to know Him and enjoy Him and obey Him and worship Him and be satisfied in Him. But we have all rebelled against that. We have all looked for fulfillment and joy in other places. We have invested our lives in the pursuit of wealth and power and pleasure. We have done whatever seemed right to us rather than what God has told us is right.

And so now we are God's enemies. We are rebels against Him and He is a threat to our way of life. He stands between me and my desire to run my world the way that I want to. And every time I decide to live my way instead of under Jesus' rule, I am wishing He did not exist; that He were dead.

Do you think you would have been different from the people in the crowd that day? Can you hear your own voice calling for Jesus' death? I can see my own face in that mob. The tragedy of our race is that every human being has divine blood on their hands. The wonder of history is that the divine Son shed His blood for this same human race.

You are Barabbas

Barabbas is famous for being the man who was set free instead of Jesus. We only know a few things about him. We know his name. Barabbas means "son of the father" (*bar*="son", *abba*="father"). Some early manuscripts of the Gospel of Matthew tell us that Barabbas' full name was Jesus Barabbas.

We also know that he was in jail, having been found guilty of starting a riot and committing a murder. He was a dangerous criminal, a killer.

Barabbas is the opposite of the people we'd like to be, and like to think of ourselves as. But for a moment, put yourself in his shoes. You are sitting in a Roman jail awaiting your death. You know you will be crucified for your crimes. And, in your more honest moments, you know you deserve it. There aren't many worse ways to die. And so day after day you sit in this jail, anticipating the nails, the mockery, the excruciating pain, the blood filling your lungs, the breaking of your legs. That's your future. You don't know when it's coming, but you know it is coming.

And then on this fateful day you hear a mob outside. Something is going on. Has word gotten out that today is your day, your day to die? It sounds like it: you can hear the crowd screaming: "Crucify him! Crucify him!"

Imagine what you'd be thinking! Finally, the Roman guards come and get you. They drag you out in front of the angry mob and... you are set completely free.

As you stand there, you watch another man stumble off under the weight of the cross—the cross you'd pictured yourself carrying. You discover as you ask some bystanders that it was Him they'd demanded be crucified; it was Him the shouts were directed at, not you. You ask what He's done, but the people near you are surprisingly hazy on that. But they chose you to live, they say, and Him to die. Somehow, you are going free because that man is going to die.

Jesus bore the guilt and shame and curse and disgrace and death that Barabbas deserved, while Barabbas received the release, the freedom, the life that Jesus deserved. Barabbas was now a free and innocent man as far as the law was concerned. Jesus was the condemned one.

You really *are* just like Barabbas! You and I are sinners; we sit in a spiritual prison, bound helpless, awaiting the day where we get the just punishment that we deserve. But then Jesus goes off to the cross in our place. He gets what we deserve: we get what He deserves.

This is the glory of the cross; that God the Father sent God the Son to die for men and women like Barabbas; men and women like us.

Why Jesus Died

Ultimately, Jesus didn't die because Pilate was weak. He didn't die because the religious leaders hated Him. He died because you and I are weak and because we have hated Him in our hearts, and because He loves us. We won't grasp the events of Good Friday unless we stand in Barabbas' shoes, and find that they fit us.

What story do you live in? What story do you use to make sense of your life? Maybe your story is that you have been dealt a bad hand in life, or that you are the victim of other people's actions, or that you would be a hero if others would just give you a chance. Or maybe your story is that you've worked hard and figured things out and so you deserve the good life that you currently enjoy. And maybe there's an element of truth to some of that.

But the Bible tells a fundamentally different story. It tells us that we are all rebels against God, and that when God came to earth, we banded together in cowardice and anger and envy to kill Him. And so the real hero of our story came to save us and deliver us from ourselves. Jesus stood in our place; He took what we deserved. And now that He's done it, we are free and able to live differently. Our chains have been removed; we are no longer God's enemies. Life is now ours to live for God's glory, free from slavery to sin and the crippling fear of what other people think of us.

If you have Jesus, then you are invited to live your life with gleeful freedom, in the light of the greatest, most exciting story imaginable. It changes everything when you live in God's story, because only there can you be truly free.

For Reflection:

- *When are you most tempted to act like Pilate?*
- *When are you most tempted to follow the crowd??*
- *Do you see yourself as fitting Barabbas' shoes? How does this make you feel?*

I see the crowd in Pilate's hall,
their furious cries I hear;
their shouts of "Crucify!" appall,
their curses fill mine ear.
And of that shouting multitude
I feel that I am one,
and in that din of voices rude
I recognize my own.

I see the scourgers rend the flesh
of God's beloved Son;
and as they smite I feel afresh
that I of them am one.
Around the cross the throng I see
that mock the sufferer's groan,
yet still my voice it seems to be,
as if I mocked alone.

'Twas I that shed that sacred blood,
I nailed him to the tree,
I crucified the Christ of God,
I joined the mockery.
Yet not the less that blood avails
to cleanse me from sin,
and not the less that cross prevails
to give me peace within.

"I See the Crowd in Pilate's Hall" by Horatius Bonar

CHAPTER SIX

THE LONG WALK

²⁶ As they led him away, they seized Simon from Cyrene, who was on his way in from the country, and put the cross on him and made him carry it behind Jesus. ²⁷ A large number of people followed him, including women who mourned and wailed for him. ²⁸ Jesus turned and said to them, "Daughters of Jerusalem, do not weep for me; weep for yourselves and for your children. ²⁹ For the time will come when you will say, 'Blessed are the barren women, the wombs that never bore and the breasts that never nursed!' ³⁰ Then 'they will say to the mountains, "Fall on us!" and to the hills, "Cover us!"' ³¹ For if men do these things when the tree is green, what will happen when it is dry?"   Luke 23 v 26-31

You've probably heard the expression that "a friend in need is a friend indeed". There's something about times of adversity that show us who we can trust. If you are rich or popular or successful or wildly good-looking (or all of the above), it's hard to know whether people are loyal to you or to the benefits you can bring to them. But when you are at your lowest and when there's nothing to gain from being associated with you, that's when you can tell who your friends really are.

As Jesus makes His way along the road to His crucifixion, He is very near to His lowest moment. He has been through a brutal night. In the Garden of Gethsemane He has looked

His fate squarely in the eye. He has tasted the cup of God's wrath that He will drink on the cross. He has been betrayed, abandoned, mocked, spat upon, beaten brutally, tried, found innocent, and condemned to death anyway.

But along the way He is accompanied by a group of women who will not leave Him, even in the time of His greatest humiliation.

Jesus and the Women

As Jesus labors down the path to the cross, He is followed by a great crowd (Luke 23 v 27). These may be some of the same people who were clamoring for His death before Pilate a few minutes before, now heading out to observe the gruesome spectacle. But Luke relates that there is also a group of women who are following along, mourning and lamenting for Him.

It's worth pausing here to notice the very positive role that women play in Luke's narrative. One of the objections that people have to biblical Christianity is that it is patriarchal, that it oppresses women and institutionalizes their subjugation. And it is true that the Bible doesn't map squarely onto the tenets of modern feminism, with its idea that there are no distinctions between men and women. The Bible teaches that men and women are both created in God's image, alike in dignity and value. It also teaches that men and women have different roles and are called to different functions in the church and in the family.

But it never, ever says that women are in any way less valuable than men.

In fact, if you look at all four Gospel accounts, you will see that Jesus faces constant opposition, sneering and harassment. But you will search in vain for one woman who is hostile to Jesus. That is remarkable! Women are portrayed much more positively than men are.

If you are a woman, you can be encouraged by the honored place that women played in the life of Jesus and in the early church. The Bible never thinks of women as second-class citizens or anything less than essential parts of the body of Christ. And if you are a man, the Bible gives you absolutely no right to treat women poorly. Jesus loved women; Luke loved women; the early church honored women. You simply are not a godly man if you don't love, honor, and cherish women.

This is powerful evidence that Luke and the other Gospel writers were not writing propaganda. They were after the truth. In a culture where women were treated with very little respect, where no rabbi would care to have a female student, it is significant that all of the Gospel writers relate the fact that Jesus honored women. There is no way that Luke would make this up. If he were trying to write a mythical account of Jesus' life that would attract new converts, this isn't where he'd go with it. There's only one possible motivation for this information being in Luke's account. It was the truth, and Luke wrote the truth.

Don't Cry for Me

As this group of women walk along the road, they weep and mourn for Jesus. But then Jesus tells them not to weep for Him, but instead to weep for themselves.

That's strange, because in a sense it is perfectly appropriate for them to weep for Jesus. Here is an innocent man, the anointed Savior sent from God, about to be murdered, slowly and publicly. This is the greatest injustice in human history. The proper human emotion in response to this event is sorrow and grief. And so the women are simply doing what seems right, and in doing so they're fulfilling the prophesy in Zechariah 12 v 10:

> When they look on me, on him whom they have pierced, they shall mourn for him, as one mourns for an only child, and weep bitterly over him, as one weeps over a firstborn. (ESV translation)

But Jesus tells them that they should be weeping for *themselves*—because, as He explains in Luke 23 v 29-31, awful days are coming. In the days ahead, women will bless those who have the privilege of being barren. Now, in that culture childlessness was seen as one of the worst things that could happen to someone. But in the coming days things will be so bad that even barrenness is preferable. It's better not to endure this kind of ordeal with children.

In verse 30, Jesus quotes to the ladies from the prophet Hosea. This is a significant reference for us if we're going to understand what Jesus is talking about. In Hosea 10 v 8, the LORD is speaking to the people of Israel about a coming day when they would be destroyed:

> The high places of wickedness will be destroyed—it is the sin of Israel. Thorn and thistle will grow up and cover their altars. Then they will say to the mountains, "Cover us!" and to the hills, "Fall on us!"

This prophecy was fulfilled when the Assyrian armies over-ran Israel in the years leading up to 722 BC (at that point God's people lived in two states; one called Israel and the other, the area around Jerusalem, called Judah), and took the people of Israel off into captivity.

Why does Jesus choose to bring that prophecy to the minds of these women at this exact moment? Well, perhaps He is warning them about the upcoming destruction of Jerusalem. Jesus has already declared that the city will be destroyed (Luke 21 v 6); and in fact, Roman armies attacked the city in AD70 in response to a Jewish uprising, and leveled Jerusalem with cruelty and violence. It was an act of destruction and judgment which paralleled the event that Hosea foretold for ancient Israel. That makes sense in light of 23 v 31, which is a saying that means something like: "If the Romans do this to me who is innocent, how much worse will it be when they come for you who are sinners?"

But there seems to be more going on in Hosea's words, and Jesus' quoting of them, than first meets the eye. After all, it seems like a strange moment for Jesus to bring up a disaster that won't happen for another 40 years. Many of these women will be dead by then.

In fact, Jesus has a different horizon in mind. The book of Revelation applies Hosea's prophecy to a different moment in history—to the end of the world, when God's wrath is fully revealed:

> There was a great earthquake. The sun turned black like sackcloth made of goat hair, the whole moon turned blood red, and the stars in the sky fell to earth, as late figs drop from a fig tree when shaken by a strong wind. The sky receded like a scroll, rolling up, and every mountain and island was removed from its place.
>
> Then the kings of the earth, the princes, the generals, the rich, the mighty, and every slave and every free man hid in caves and among the rocks of the mountains. They called to the mountains and the rocks, "Fall on us and hide us from the face of him who sits on the throne and from the wrath of the Lamb! For the great day of their wrath has come, and who can stand?"   (Revelation 6 v 12-17)

Hosea's prophecy refers not just to a temporal, physical destruction, but also to an end-time experience of God's wrath. When we put it all together, Jesus is telling these women to weep for themselves because they are going to experience something so awful that it should move them to horrified tears. It's not merely the fall of Jerusalem that He is talking about. That is a terrible event, something that no one would want to live through. But Jesus is looking to something far worse. He's talking about the judgment that awaits them at the end of time. That day will be a day of fierce wrath from an opponent who is far worse than even the Roman army.

These well-meaning women don't understand the big picture. They weep for Jesus because they see that He is condemned. In the words of Isaiah 53, they can see that He is stricken, smitten by God, and afflicted. What they don't understand is that they are under the same curse. They are under the same condemnation. They are going to experience a day of judgment that will bring them face to face with the wrath of God, just as Jesus is walking to face it on the cross. They are no better off than Him. If they realized what that day of judgment will be like, they would weep for themselves.

The True Friend Indeed

These women were truly faithful friends to Jesus in His time of need, "friends indeed" in the terms of the old saying we mentioned earlier. But the deeper reality is that it was Jesus who was their true friend. Their hour of spiritual need was pressing upon them, and as Jesus walked off to give His life for their sake, it was He who was the true friend indeed.

And if Jesus says this to these women, these tender women who have compassion on Him here when no one else will, He is most certainly saying it to us as well. God does not play around with justice. You and I will face a perfectly holy Judge on that last day; and it will be awful.

God's fierce hatred for sin and rebellion is such that when we face that day we will beg for the mountains to crush us so that we can be hidden from God. We have all got a date with the wrath of God.

And so what does Jesus tell these women (and us!) to do? They should weep for themselves and for the fate of their children. So should you; you ought to consider carefully what will happen to you on that day. Think about what will happen, and then weep. Not tears of pity, but tears of repentance. This is the only way to prepare for that last day; you must see the severity of your sin, see how you have offended God, see that you deserve His eternal punishment, and then repent. Turn from your sin.

Do you take your sin seriously? Do you think that it is a small thing that you have rebelled against your Creator, the God who made you and to whom you owe complete and perfect obedience? You may excuse your faults and failures: your temper, your bad habits, your disrespect, your pride, your immorality. But God does not. If we don't care about our sin, that is simply evidence of how deeply ingrained our rebellion is, and how deserved our judgment will be. The right response, the only sensible response, is to weep.

Jesus and the Stranger

John's Gospel tells us that as Jesus was led away, He was bearing His own cross (John 19 v 17). This was a common practice. The Romans knew how to get the maximum bang for their buck, and so it wasn't enough for them to kill criminals and rebels in a horrible fashion; they wanted to make a point. And so it was the custom to make the condemned man carry the cross piece of the cross, called the *patibulum*, through the streets of the town. It was a method of spreading terror and keeping the people in line, as if to say: "This is what happens to people who oppose Rome!"

But it seems that at some point in the journey Jesus is not able to carry it any further. That's not a surprise, given the ordeal that He has been through. But since it's no good to crucify someone if you kill them on the way, the guards grab a man named Simon from Cyrene in North Africa and make him carry the cross-piece for Jesus. Simon is on his way in from the country on this fateful day, presumably minding his own business, when he is suddenly pressed into service.

Carrying a Cross

Luke doesn't tell us that Jesus and Simon had any conversation about what was happening. But Christians have often noticed that there is a certain appropriateness in the event. Every follower of Jesus is a bit like Simon of Cyrene in that we're called to carry the cross and follow Jesus (Luke 9 v 23).

The pattern of the Christian life is a radical death to oneself, a radical identification with Jesus' death and crucifixion. Simon of Cyrene is a vivid reminder of the truth that following Jesus means going with Him on the path to the cross. Following Jesus, being with Jesus, requires you to come and pick up your cross and die.

This happens to everyone when they become a Christian. The Bible speaks of us as already dead to sin, already crucified with Jesus. In Galatians 2 v 20, Paul wrote: "I have been crucified with Christ and I no longer live, but Christ lives in me". And in Galatians 5 v 24, he said: "Those who belong to Christ Jesus have crucified the sinful nature with its passions and desires".

There is a very real sense in which we are no longer under slavery to sin; we no longer have to do its will; we now live for Christ. We don't make this death happen, but the Bible calls us to look to this death and to remember it.

But there is another sense in which the Bible talks about our death to sin as something that *we* must do. We deny ourselves. By the power of the Spirit, we turn our back on ourselves. In repentance, we renounce our right to control our own fate and do whatever we want. This is what it means to pick up your cross, and this is something that, according to Jesus, must be done daily. It's not a box to be checked once and then forgotten. It's a daily death.

The cross of Christ makes demands of us. It will not allow us to love the world *and* love Christ. It will not permit half-hearted devotion. If Christ is to live in you, sin and selfishness must be put to death.

So what would it look like for you to pick up *your* cross?

Perhaps there is flagrant, sinful behavior that must stop. In this way, picking up your cross daily is simply repentance and walking in obedience. It's grabbing a hammer and nails (metaphorically speaking) and taking your cherished sins and nailing them to the cross.

Or perhaps there is some comfort that you must forego. To follow Jesus is to follow Him to the cross. It is to sign up to be an outsider in many ways to the world's system. It's to bear the reproach that He endured. There is a very real danger that we begin our Christian lives well, and we're repentant and we're willing. But over time we start to think as if Jesus is merely a provider of religious goods and services. We begin to pray as if Jesus is a genie in the sky. We begin to be angry if things don't go the way that we think is best. We become resentful if we have to suffer even minor inconveniences.

But like Simon, we are called to carry the cross. It means that the way to life is through a daily death to ourselves and our sin. We are called to suffer for the sake of Christ. The call to follow Christ is a call to come and die.

Whose Cross is it Anyway?

Simon of Cyrene is a reminder to us that we must carry the cross (metaphorically, spiritually) as he did literally. But if we think that's all that's going on here, then we misunderstand what is happening on the road to Calvary.

We shouldn't look at Simon, helping Jesus here at a moment of physical failure, and think that by "carrying our cross" we're somehow helping Jesus out. That's not how this works. When we deny ourselves and pick up our cross, we are not helping Jesus. We are not giving Him an assist in His work of salvation. We don't carry the ball as far as we can and then Jesus takes it over the goal line for us.

As Simon assists Jesus with the burden of the cross beam, it's possible to lose perspective and forget the big picture. The big picture is that Jesus is stumbling along that road in order to help Simon. Jesus is in a moment of intense need, and Simon helps Him. But again, just like the women who wept for Jesus, *Simon* is the one in the greatest need. Jesus is enduring all of this as a faithful friend to sinners like Simon. Though Jesus is in need, He is again the true friend indeed.

We need to look at Simon and see what Jesus has done for us. Like you and me, Simon was a rebel against a holy God. The fact that he had lived this many years enjoying life in Cyrene (or wherever else he had lived) was far more than he deserved. He would have had no right to complain to God if God had given him justice for his sins right then and there. And so we must realize that Simon wasn't really carrying Jesus' cross. *He was carrying his own.*

I usually read this story and think: "How unfair that the Roman soldiers made this innocent bystander bear this awful burden". But there was only one innocent man there that day! And the fact that Simon eventually got to put that cross beam down and that they nailed Jesus to it is the real amazing injustice.

That cross beam on Simon's shoulders was simply a brief and momentary reminder of the weight of the condemnation that he carried around every day of his life. We all live under a death sentence; there is a cross beam firmly fixed on the shoulders of every human being on the planet. There is one on you right now, whether you can see it or not. Simon just had the opportunity to have it made visible to him for a brief time.

So, what do you think happened to Simon after he carried the cross for Jesus? Do you think that he carried the cross to the crucifixion site, put it down, and then went about his business back in town? I think we can be confident that he did not. After all, Luke refers to him as "Simon from Cyrene", which makes it seem he was known to Luke's audience (as in: "Which Simon?" "You know, Simon from Cyrene"). In addition, we know from Mark 15 v 21 that Simon's two sons, Alexander and Rufus, were also well known to the early church.

Where do you think Alexander and Rufus heard about Jesus? Presumably it's not down to a cosmic coincidence that years later they ran into someone who told them about Jesus, this crucified rabbi whose cross their dad had carried. It seems pretty clear that their father must have told them about Him.

Simon had presumably never heard of Jesus. He was just a foreigner walking into town one afternoon when his life took an amazing turn. That day he got a close-up, insider look at this most amazing event. He heard Jesus speak to these weeping women along the road. He probably listened as Jesus cried out: "Father, forgive them, for they do not know what they are doing" (Luke 23 v 34); saw the sky go dark; heard about the curtain in the temple tearing in two (v 44-45). And it changed him forever. How kind of God to allow Simon to be burdened, to be inconvenienced, to be imposed upon in this way so that he might be brought to see the Savior!

The events of these couple of hours transformed Simon and the fate of his family. The sight of Jesus on the cross changed the course of this man's life... and it will change ours. It reminds us of the need for repentance and the need to deny ourselves and carry our cross. But it also shows us that we will never be able to do those things unless we have seen Jesus on His cross, until we have understood what He has done for us, until we grasp that He is the friend indeed, taking our cross beam from our shoulders.

The cross that Jesus bore was not His own; it was ours. If you get that in place, then the tears will come, the repentance will come, and picking up your cross daily and following after Him will be the only possible response.

For Reflection:

- *Has the truth that Jesus bore your cross changed your life? How (or how should it)?*

- *What do you need to repent of? How do these thoughts, words or deeds make you feel as you look at the cross?*

- *How does Jesus' love for you motivate you to carry a cross to follow Him? In what ways is He calling you to do this?*

Jesus, I my cross have taken,
All to leave and follow Thee.
Destitute, despised, forsaken,
Thou from hence my all shall be.
Perish every fond ambition,
All I've sought or hoped or known.
Yet how rich is my condition!
God and heaven are still my own.

Let the world despise and leave me,
They have left my Savior too.
Human hearts and looks deceive me;
Thou art not, like them, untrue.
O while Thou dost smile upon me,
God of wisdom, love and might,
Foes may hate and friends disown me,
Show Thy face and all is bright.

Soul, then know thy full salvation
Rise o'er sin and fear and care.
Joy to find in every station,
Something still to do or bear.
Think what Spirit dwells within thee,
Think what Father's smiles are thine,
Think that Jesus died to win thee,
Child of heaven, canst thou repine.

"Jesus, I My Cross Have Taken" by Henry Lyte

CHAPTER SEVEN

FATHER, FORGIVE

³² Two other men, both criminals, were also led out with him to be executed. ³³ When they came to the place called the Skull, there they crucified him, along with the criminals—one on his right, the other on his left. ³⁴ Jesus said, "Father, forgive them, for they do not know what they are doing." And they divided up his clothes by casting lots.

³⁵ The people stood watching, and the rulers even sneered at him. They said, "He saved others; let him save himself if he is the Christ of God, the Chosen One."

³⁶ The soldiers also came up and mocked him. They offered him wine vinegar ³⁷ and said, "If you are the king of the Jews, save yourself."

³⁸ There was a written notice above him, which read: THIS IS THE KING OF THE JEWS.   Luke 23 v 32-38

Forgiveness is difficult.

On the one hand, it requires something that feels like an act of injustice. Imagine that someone has done something wrong to you; perhaps they have slandered you or lied to you or stolen from you. Forgiveness in that case can seem somehow wrong, almost like a lie. If you forgive that person, it's as if you're saying that what they did never really happened, or at least wasn't really that bad. But that thing did happen, and it did hurt; and so forgiveness feels wrong.

But on the other hand, forgiveness is absolutely necessary. Because, let's face it, if there were no forgiveness the world would grind to a halt. All of us do things that are wrong. Even the best of us hurt and offend others in some ways. At some point, all of us will need forgiveness. If no one ever forgave anyone else, we'd be in permanent gridlock. No one could be happily married, or have close friends, or have a good relationship with their parents. And holding onto a grudge is simply exhausting. It takes a lot of energy to be unforgiving, even though some people manage to keep it up for years.

So the whole notion of forgiveness raises a lot of challenging questions:

- Who should be forgiven?
- Are there things that are unforgiveable?
- What kind of apology should be required before someone is forgiven? Must it be sincere?
- Should there be a prolonged pattern of changed behavior before you forgive someone?
- Can you forgive someone unilaterally, even if they don't ask for it?

And what about God? He's never done anything for which He has needed to ask forgiveness, but He has endured wrong from each and every one of us. None of us has been faithful to Him; we've ignored Him and even blamed Him for our mistakes and problems. And what's more, God says that because He loves what (or rather, who) He's made, He also takes personal offense at all of the things that we do to other people. As the Creator and Sustainer of all people,

God says that He is an offended party in all of our sin. Every time we sin against another person, we sin against God as well.

I think that naturally we quite like (scratch that, we *rely on*) the idea of a God who forgives us, and those we love; and deep down we find it hard, or even hateful, to think of a God who is willing to forgive everyone, including the people who have hurt us deeply or who have scarred humanity globally.

So, should God forgive? If so, who should God forgive? Under what circumstances? How can God forgive terrible things without being unjust?

These are questions of eternal and daily relevance to our lives. And they're questions that were at the forefront of Jesus' mind, even as His body was nailed to a cross by the humanity that He'd come to love.

The Unsaved Savior

We have seen throughout the narrative of Jesus' trial that there is an ironic fulfillment of the words of Jesus' enemies. And again we see it here. It was normal to have a placard above the condemned man listing his crimes. An inscription is placed over Jesus that says: "The king of the Jews" (Luke 23 v 38). John tells us that the sign was Pilate's idea (John 19 v 19). Pilate had found Jesus innocent of all charges; so there was nothing to write on His inscription. So Pilate decided to take a little shot at the Jewish leaders. He knew it would drive them nuts to see Jesus proclaimed their king, even in the hour of His death.

The irony, of course, is that we've seen all along that this man really *is* the King of the Jews; and that it is through His cross that He reaches His throne. To all appearances, Jesus is a wretched man being murdered by a conspiracy of envious religious leaders and cruel, cowardly politicians. But far more than that is really going on. On that cross, Jesus is saving His people. It is actually by *not* saving Himself that Jesus shows himself to be the King, and reveals what kind of King He is. He is not simply being murdered; rather He is choosing to lay down His life in order to drink the cup. As Jesus hangs there in agony and blood, He is taking the punishment for the sins of His people. He is dying so that we might live.

And this is His coronation. In Philippians 2 v 8-10, Paul connects Jesus' suffering to His regal glory:

> And being found in human form, he humbled himself by becoming obedient to the point of death, even death on a cross. Therefore God has highly exalted him and bestowed on him the name that is above every name, so that at the name of Jesus every knee should bow, in heaven and on earth and under the earth, and every tongue confess that Jesus Christ is Lord, to the glory of God the Father. (ESV)

The words of Jesus' enemies are turned back on them. "He saved others; let him save himself if he is the Christ," they sneer (Luke 23 v 35); but in fact, Jesus shows His kingship by *not* saving Himself.

The rulers' words would be comical, if they weren't so tragic. They freely acknowledge that Jesus "saved others", that He performed miracles and healings, but they still won't believe in Him. Again, their words are pregnant with unintentional truth. The fact is, there is one person Jesus cannot save. He can either save you, or He can save Himself. He can either die in your place so that you might go free, or He can save Himself and leave you to perish.

And He chose to save you.

Father, Condemn

What would you say if you were in Jesus' situation? What would be in your mind and on your lips? Would you be thirsting for revenge against the people who had done this to you? Be overwhelmed by the sheer unfairness of it all? Scream silent curses at the people who had gathered to taunt you? Plot to wipe the smug looks off their faces, and look forward to the day when they would eat their words? Those are pretty close to what I'd be feeling and saying.

In verse 34, nailed to a cross, Jesus speaks. He has limited time left. He needs to choose His words carefully. What does He say?

"Father, forgive them, for they do not know what they are doing."

These words almost defy any further comment. There is Jesus hanging on the cross, in deep agony, His life ebbing away—and His concern is for His tormentors. He cares about the fact that they are heaping up condemnation and damnation for themselves. And so He prays for their forgiveness, adding that they don't know what they are doing.

Who is Jesus praying for here? Some have suggested that He is praying for the Roman soldiers, who have just entered into the story and genuinely have no way of knowing who it is that they are crucifying. Some say He is praying for the crowd, many of whom were swept up in the moment and presumably had not stopped to think carefully about what they were doing. But there's no reason why Jesus is not including everyone present there, even the Jewish leaders who have deliberately pursued Him to the cross.

In a sense, they know what they are doing, but in a very real way they have no idea what kind of terrible crime they are committing. They think they are doing God a service by killing this Jesus; they have suppressed the truth about who they are killing to the extent that they are unable to know that truth even in a small corner of their hearts. They have gone so far that they are incapable of seeing that they are, in fact, heaping condemnation on themselves. And so Jesus prays that the Father would enable them to see what they are doing, realize their crime, and turn to Him in repentance so that He might forgive them.

But there's still a problem. It's inconceivable that these people could be forgiven for their crime. They are killing an innocent man. They are adding to His suffering by their taunting and abuse. It makes no sense that a just and holy God would wipe that slate clean. In fact, justice demands that He doesn't.

But that's the wonder of the cross. On the cross, God the Father placed on His Son Jesus the sins of all His people. At the cross, Jesus died not in mere physical agony, but in spiritual agony as He drank the cup, as He took the justice our sins against God deserved. Jesus paid the price for all of the selfishness, greed, envy, anger, cowardice, laziness and foolishness that stood round that cross. He took the death sentence that He alone did not deserve. God Himself paid the price for everyone else there that day, for everyone throughout the world who was alive that day and every day. Jesus did not only ask for people to be forgiven; He made it possible for them to be forgiven.

Have you ever stopped to appreciate how strongly Jesus desired to forgive people? He went to Jerusalem, despite knowing what was going to happen to Him there (Luke 18 v 31-34). No matter how many times His disciples let Him down, no matter how many times people rejected Him, no matter how many times the religious leaders tried to destroy Him, He kept on going to Jerusalem. He kept on walking towards the cross where He would give up His life to offer forgiveness.

It's amazing that Jesus did that for the people of His day, and it's amazing that Jesus did that for us. God's Son knew what we would turn out to be like, He knew all of our failures and sins and weaknesses; and He died for us anyway. He wanted to forgive us so much that He deliberately walked towards His death.

Forgiveness always comes at a cost. For God's Son, it came at the cost of His own life.

The Forgiving Life of the Forgiven

How can you forgive guilty people? Forgiveness presents us with a problem, but the cross of Christ is God's solution. It is the solution which means that we can be forgiven; it is also the solution to the conundrum of us forgiving others. Put simply, if we know we are forgiven by God through the cross, we will forgive others no matter what they have done, no matter how high the cost.

We need to feel the power of a parable Jesus told on His way to Jerusalem:

> The kingdom of heaven is like a king who wanted to settle accounts with his servants. As he began the settlement, a man who owed him ten thousand talents was brought to him. Since he was not able to pay, the master ordered that he and his wife and his children and all that he had be sold to repay the debt.
>
> The servant fell on his knees before him. "Be patient with me," he begged, "and I will pay back everything." The servant's master took pity on him, canceled the debt and let him go.
>
> But when that servant went out, he found one of his fellow servants who owed him a hundred denarii. He grabbed him and began to

choke him. "Pay back what you owe me!" he demanded.

His fellow servant fell to his knees and begged him, "Be patient with me, and I will pay you back."

But he refused. Instead, he went off and had the man thrown into prison until he could pay the debt. When the other servants saw what had happened, they were greatly distressed and went and told their master everything that had happened.

Then the master called the servant in. "You wicked servant," he said, "I canceled all that debt of yours because you begged me to. Shouldn't you have had mercy on your fellow servant just as I had on you?" In anger his master turned him over to the jailers to be tortured, until he should pay back all he owed.

This is how my heavenly Father will treat each of you unless you forgive your brother from your heart.   (Matthew 18 v 23-35)

Jesus' point is clear: if you have been forgiven by God, you *will* be forgiving towards others. To put it the other way around—if we won't forgive, we show we haven't really understood that we need forgiveness ourselves, and found it through the cross.

To feel the full force of what Jesus is saying here, we need to know that the debt that the second servant owed to the first was significant (over $10,000, or £6,500, in our terms). That's a lot of money! It wasn't an easy thing to write off. To cancel the debt would cost the first servant dearly.

But the first servant also owed a sum of money—an amount far, far greater (six thousand million dollars, or almost four thousand million pounds). Compared to that, the amount he was owed by the second servant suddenly seems very insignificant! Someone who had been forgiven so much should have been able to forgive his debtors.

In the same way, the costly forgiveness that Christ offers must transform the way that we think about the sin others commit against us. However hurt we are, however repeated the sin against us, however costly forgiving someone would be, it is nowhere near what God has forgiven us, and what God goes on forgiving us.

Is there someone in your life that you simply feel you cannot forgive? Maybe it's a raw, fresh wound. Maybe its decades of simmering animosity towards a spouse who hasn't been what you wanted, a sort of low-grade fever that you don't even notice anymore. Maybe it's an open wound that hurts everyday. I assume the other person doesn't deserve your forgiveness; that's how this works. If you look at that wrong you have been done, it will seem too great to cancel. If you look at the cross and see it in the light of Jesus' forgiveness of you, it will seem too small not to forgive. Whatever—*whatever*—it is, the Christian must, and can, look to the cross and forgive.

Personally, I don't find it hard to forgive most things. By temperament I'm pretty laid-back and most things roll off my back. But there is one particular person in my past that I genuinely struggle to forgive. I feel so wronged by this person and the things that they have done, and they are so unrepentant, it just seems impossible to let them off the hook of my angry heart.

But I must remember that this person's sin against me doesn't begin to compare to my sin against God. The things that I have suffered at this person's hand are nothing compared to what Christ suffered for my sake. This person owes me, big time; but I owe God infinitely, and He's forgiven it all. It doesn't come naturally to me, and I don't find it easy, but as I look at the Son of God on His cross, thinking of me and saying: "Father, forgive", how can I possibly refuse to forgive?

The Father who Forgives

Forgiveness actually lies at the heart of God's dealings with His people. It's not as though Jesus, as He was hoisted up on His cross, said: "Father, forgive", and His Father suddenly realized this was a great idea and wished He'd thought of it before. The idea of forgiveness is the Father's, and always has been.

When, over a thousand years before Jesus died, Moses asked to see God's glory—what it is that makes God God— the Creator told him what lies at the heart of His Godness:

> The LORD, the LORD, the compassionate and gracious God, slow to anger, abounding in love and faithfulness, maintaining love to thousands, and forgiving wickedness, rebellion and sin. Yet he does not leave the guilty unpunished. (Exodus 34 v 6-7)

With that in mind, it's instructive for us to pause and take stock of what exactly Luke has pulled out for us see in the crucifixion. He can't tell us everything that happened; he must choose carefully what details he thinks we need to know in order to understand what happened to Jesus. So first, notice what he doesn't tell us. He doesn't talk about the pain. Verse 33 simply relates the facts: "They crucified him". No long, gory descriptions of the suffering. No brutal explanations of how the human anatomy fails in these circumstances.

Instead, Luke pulls out three specific details that show how the events surrounding Jesus' crucifixion serve to fulfill Old Testament prophecy. This is important, because it's reminding us about God's character. It's showing us that the forgiveness the Son offers at the cross is the heart of the Father's eternal plan. First, in verse 32 Jesus is crucified between two criminals, whose forgiveness He then prays for. Hundreds of years earlier, the prophet Isaiah had said that this very thing would happen to the servant of the Lord:

> He poured out his life unto death, and was numbered with the
> transgressors. For he bore the sin of many, and made intercession
> for the transgressors. (Isaiah 53 v 12)

The second fulfillment comes in verse 34, where the soldiers cast lots to divide Jesus' garments. People were crucified naked to add to the humiliation and pain, and it was a common practice that the clothing of the condemned man belonged to the executioners. So they gamble to decide who got what. What they can't know is that in doing so at the foot of this particular cross, they are fulfilling words written a thousand years earlier:

> They divide my garments among them and cast lots for my
> clothing. (Psalm 22 v 18)

Third, as we've seen, in verse 35 the rulers gather around Jesus to taunt Him. In verse 36 the soldiers join in, mocking Him with their words and with an offer of vinegar to quench His thirst. Can you imagine the cruelty and contempt that it would take for someone to act this way, to taunt an innocent man who is in agony? But again, the unwitting fulfillment of prophecy is clear. In another part of Psalm 22, David cried out:

> All who see me mock me; they hurl insults, shaking their heads:
> "He trusts in the LORD; let the LORD rescue him ... since he delights
> in him" ... Dogs have surrounded me; a band of evil men has encir-
> cled me, they have pierced my hands and my feet. I can count all
> my bones; people stare and gloat over me.
>
> (Psalm 22 v 7-8, 16-17)

Here, David speaks words that were true in his own life-situation, but it becomes clear that God's Spirit was also speaking through him of a future day and a future experience of Jesus, a future King of Israel.

God had described hundreds of years before, in intricate detail, what would take place in the crucifixion of Christ. Jesus is the point of the whole Bible. He didn't just drop out of the sky and begin His ministry. No, the story of Jesus starts back at the beginning of the Old Testament. The story of Israel is the story of God preparing the ground for His Messiah, the one who would offer forgiveness to the world. The message of the Old Testament is a message of promise, fulfilled in the crucifixion and resurrection of Jesus.

Everything that happened to Jesus was completely ordained by God. It must be so. How else could God speak a word to Isaiah or through David and have it fulfilled hundreds of years later? It can only be because He's the one who makes it happen. God's word is always fulfilled because He is the one in control of the events that fulfill it.

That means that we should stop and appreciate the amazing love on display here. Sometimes we talk about the "godhead"—Father, Son, Spirit—in an unhelpful way. It's easy to get the impression that God the Father is super-holy and angry about our sin, but Jesus is loving and so He died for us to save us from the Father, forcing the Father to forgive. But that can't be true, because we see the whole plan of salvation, the entire rescue mission, was at God's initiative. God delights in it; He's been talking about it throughout the whole Old Testament. The cross is His plan, His initiative:

> For God [the Father] so loved the world that he gave his one and
> only Son, that whoever believes in him shall not perish but have
> eternal life. (John 3 v 16)

God is a God who forgives. Not because (in the words of the 19th-century German poet Heinrich Heine) it's His job, as if the Father is compelled to forgive by some power outside Himself. No—God freely forgives because of who He is. Forgiveness isn't His job; it's His character. The Father sent His Son to bear His justice because He's a God who forgives.

The point here is not that when someone wrongs us, we should suck it up and begrudgingly forgive them because it's the right thing to do. No, the challenge is for us to love God more, to be more amazed by His love for us, and to be more and more enthralled with a Savior who would do this for us despite, and because of, our sin against Him.

As we come to love God more, as we come to treasure Jesus more highly, as we come to appreciate the eternal debt that He canceled in His death, we will become more like Him. We'll start to live and act like children of our heavenly Father. We will really be able to forgive others as we have been forgiven, and we'll love to be able to do for others what God has done for us. We'll be able to connect the dots as we pray the "Lord's Prayer". We'll ask God—Father, Son and Spirit—to do what He loves to do as we say: "Forgive us our debts". And then we'll really mean, and love, and live by, the next phrase: "as we also have forgiven our debtors" (Matthew 6 v 12, ESV).

For Reflection:

- *Do you tend to see yourself as someone who has been wronged, or as someone who needs forgiveness?*
- *How do Jesus' words and actions on the cross encourage and challenge your own forgiveness of others?*
- *Is there someone you need to forgive?*

What can wash away my sin?
Nothing but the blood of Jesus;
What can make me whole again?
Nothing but the blood of Jesus.

For my pardon, this I see,
Nothing but the blood of Jesus;
For my cleansing, this my plea,
Nothing but the blood of Jesus.

Nothing can for sin atone,
Nothing but the blood of Jesus;
Naught of good that I have done,
Nothing but the blood of Jesus.

This is all my hope and peace,
Nothing but the blood of Jesus;
This is all my righteousness,
Nothing but the blood of Jesus.

"Nothing but the Blood of Jesus" by Robert Lowry

CHAPTER EIGHT

TWO CRIMINALS

³⁹ One of the criminals who hung there hurled insults at him: "Aren't you the Christ? Save yourself and us!"

⁴⁰ But the other criminal rebuked him. "Don't you fear God," he said, "since you are under the same sentence? ⁴¹ We are punished justly, for we are getting what our deeds deserve. But this man has done nothing wrong."

⁴² Then he said, "Jesus, remember me when you come into your kingdom."

⁴³ Jesus answered him, "I tell you the truth, today you will be with me in paradise."

Luke 23 v 39-43

Where does your mind drift to when you hear the word "heaven"? What do you think heaven will be like?

Maybe you think of heaven as a place where nothing bad happens and your favorite sports team always wins (as a fan of the New York Yankees, I pretty much live in this paradise already). I have a friend who jokes that heaven will be an endless buffet of Mexican food, just without the calories and indigestion!

Or perhaps you think in terms of the old cartoon vision of heaven: baby angels in diapers, people floating on clouds in white dresses while playing a harp. (I don't know about you, but that doesn't sound to me like a very pleasant way to spend eternity!)

Or on a more serious note, perhaps heaven to you is a place where you'll be reunited with loved ones who have died. Maybe it's the place where you'll finally be free from the sickness, the pain, the heartache.

As Jesus hung on the cross, dying in agony in the heat of the day, abandoned by His friends and tortured by His enemies, He was about as far from heaven as any human being could possibly be. But surprisingly, His thoughts went briefly to this topic. In fact, some of the very last words He spoke before his death were about heaven. And what He said can help us shape, or reshape, our views on what it means to "go to heaven", and who it is who goes there.

Two Criminals: Two Fates

Luke's already told us that "two other men, both criminals, were also led out with [Jesus] to be executed" (23 v 32). Luke lingers far longer on these two men than any of the other Gospel writers. It stands out in his narrative, and yet we don't know much for certain about their backgrounds. The Greek word used to describe them (*lestes*) usually means "robber". But it can also mean "insurrectionist"; someone who tries to start a revolution against the government. The fact that these men are being crucified indicates that they were guilty of serious crimes against the state, something more severe than petty theft.

Remember the setting: all around the cross of Christ are scoffers and mockers. We've seen the Jewish leaders and Roman soldiers taunting Him and sneeringly challenging Him to prove that He is the King that He claimed to be. Now, one of these criminals begins to join in the chorus; as he "hung there, [he] hurled insults at him" (v 39).

This is extraordinary. This man is being crucified; and I'll spare you all the details, but the way that crucifixion worked was that it slowly suffocated you. Hanging by your arms had the effect of putting great strain on the chest and lungs. And so someone being crucified would have to lurch themselves up by putting downward pressure on the nail driven through their feet, just to get enough air to stay alive. It was, of course, very painful. But if you persisted too long in catching your breath this way, your executioners would break your legs so that you couldn't do it anymore.

So this isn't a man having a relaxed conversation sitting comfortably in his living room. To speak, this man has to push himself up on his pierced feet just long enough to catch his breath. And then once he has caught that precious breath, one of the last he will ever take, he uses it to abuse Jesus and ask Him: "Aren't you meant to be the Christ?! Then save us and save yourself!"

This man clearly doesn't think that Jesus is, or even could be, the Christ. If he did, the insults wouldn't have formed in his mind, let alone have passed his lips. He doesn't believe that Jesus is the Messiah, the chosen one, the anointed Savior sent by God. And in some ways, you can't blame him. Hanging there amid the shouts and taunts of the people, Jesus hardly looks like a king.

This is not an honest seeker. But still, the first criminal lays out the conditions which, if met, will cause him to believe in Jesus. He basically says: "Look, Jesus. Aren't you supposed to be the all-powerful King? Get yourself off your cross, then get me off mine, and then I'll believe that you are the Christ!"

He wants Jesus to prove Himself by doing him a favor: "If you do something for me, I'll (kind of) believe in you. Get me out of this mess, and I'll worship you."

Have you ever prayed a prayer like that? "God, if you do what I want, in return I will acknowledge that you exist and maybe even do some stuff for you." Of course, the unspoken flip side of that prayer is: "If you don't, I won't". Non-Christians play this game ("God, if you're there, give me a car. Or a girlfriend. Or a job."). But believers play it too. Religious people actually play it really well. We very easily end up approaching God on the basis not of what we will do, but what we have done—which is essentially the same thing. It looks like this: "God, I've already done everything I was supposed to do. I have kept the rules; I have done everything right; I deserve a good life. So now it's your turn to do something: pay me back by taking away this problem!"

But that's not how things work. In fact, Jesus could have saved this man. He could spoken a word and instantly freed this man from his cross, to get on with living his life. He could give everyone the car, the girlfriend, the job, whenever they ask. He could sort out every problem we face in the present.

But that's not the deliverance that Jesus is offering. Jesus is holding out to this man, and to every man and woman, a different kind of salvation. The whole reason that the Christ is on the cross is so that this criminal can be saved *from* judgment and *for* eternal life! But he misses that, because he's only focused on his present, because he only demands relief right here and right now. He only wants a god who gratifies him instantly, and in just the way he wants.

And Jesus is not that god.

Don't miss the implications of this fact. God is far more interested in the state of your soul than He is in delivering you from your present circumstances. In fact, it could be that He put you in your present circumstances for the good of your soul. If you have a difficulty in your life right now, a family problem or physical issue, a disappointment or a heartbreak, it is fine to ask God to take it away. It's good to seek God's help and relief. And He can help. But we mustn't make our love for and worship of Jesus conditional on Him taking away our problems. It is faithful to pray: "God, help!", but it is wretched to pray: "God, help, or else!"

As we've seen, Jesus Himself essentially prayed this on the Mount of Olives: "Take this cup of suffering away, but ultimately, let your will be done" (see 22 v 42). God is not some cosmic genie, here at your beck and call. He is more wise and good and powerful than you, so He may take things in a different direction than the one you'd prefer. We should never come to God with our list of demands. And we should never be so fixated on our present that we forget to care about our future.

Amazingly, the second criminal grasps this. He challenges his some-time partner in crime: "Don't you fear God?" (v 40). The first criminal's thoughts are consumed with mocking Jesus, rather than meeting his Maker. But the second thief realizes their greatest fear should not be the pain of the cross, but the terror of meeting God.

And the second criminal also knows that "we are punished justly, for we are getting what our deeds deserve" (v 41). Exactly what is he talking about? He could be talking about Rome, saying that he now recognizes the government's right to punish those who rebel against it and threaten the common welfare. But this is unlikely; if he were an insurrectionist, he would have longed for Rome's overthrow every day of his life, including his last. He's probably not acknowledging the justice in the death sentence handed down by the Roman authorities.

It seems much more likely that something else has happened here; that the grace of God had revealed to this man that he was under a far greater condemnation, the judgment of God. This second criminal has realized that he will soon have to give an account to a perfect God, who will give him what he deserves for everything he has ever done. And his record is not good. His death on his cross is only the beginning, not the end, of his suffering.

In Paradise

The difference between the two thieves is startling. The first criminal cares about nothing but his own present well-being; his definition of paradise seems to be getting off the cross, getting away from the Roman authorities, and going back to his old life. But the second criminal's mind is in a different place. He realizes that he is getting what he deserves on the cross, that he is under a sentence of condemnation from both the human authorities and also from God. He is not consumed with bitterness about his present fate, but instead he has begun to worry about his future. He is concerned about eternity.

And as he looks at the man hanging on the middle cross, he sees the King of eternity. So this hardened criminal, this condemned rebel, speaks to the man dying next to him and he says: "Jesus, remember me when you come into your kingdom" (v 42). He has no track record to stand on. He has no good deeds with which to seek to impress. He just asks Jesus to remember him.

And Jesus' reply is beautiful: "I tell you the truth, today you will be with me in paradise" (v 43). This criminal asks for mercy, he asks to be remembered for good... and Jesus promises him that he will be in paradise that very day. That's more than the robber dared to ask for. The word for "paradise" means "garden". It's an image of abundance, fertility, and blessing. This is the word used to refer to the Garden of Eden, the original "paradise" of life in an unspoiled world. It's everything that we are designed to enjoy, that we yearn to enjoy, and that our sin has stopped us enjoying. It's perfection.

And Jesus is its King. He has the authority to grant admission. He doesn't need to ask permission from anyone to make this promise to the thief. He has the right to let him in.

What an amazing promise to make to a man like this! He is doubtless a hard man. He would have known poverty and violence. He has been captured by the authorities, kept in an unsanitary prison, beaten for his crimes, nailed to a cross. And here, in the midst of a gruesome ending to his unpleasant life, he finds himself on his way to paradise. All because of Jesus.

This thief teaches us what we all too often forget (if we ever knew it): you don't need to do *anything* to go to heaven. Here this man simply acknowledges God's right to judge; he accepts that he deserves condemnation for his sins; and he asks Jesus to help him. And he is promised life in paradise.

So it can't be true that you have to be good enough to go to heaven. It can't be true that you must be baptized, or be a member of a particular type of church, in order to be saved. It can't be true that you must accumulate a certain amount of merit of your own, or that you must do certain things, in order to keep the salvation that Jesus has given you. Instead, in order to be saved you must realize the two things that this repentant thief did: that he was a great sinner, and that Jesus was a great Savior.

All this man brings to the equation is his sin, his shame and his request. And that's all anyone needs in order to be saved: sorrowful repentance and humble trust. He has the audacity to ask Jesus for everything without anything to offer in return, and Jesus gives it to him! We should all be, and can all be, so bold.

This also helps to answer the question: "What happens to you when you die?" Jesus promises this man immediate entrance into paradise. No purgatory to work off some of his sins. No soul sleep, waiting for a future day. Jesus tells him that he will be in paradise that very day. If you are a believer in Christ, when you die you go to heaven, you go to paradise. Your body, like the body of this thief, will be buried and await the resurrection of the dead on the Day of Judgment. But your soul will go to be in the presence of God.

With Me

It's an amazing promise: today you will be in paradise. But that's not the best promise in verse 43. We tend to put the emphasis on the wrong words. We tend to read the words this way: Today you'll be with me *in paradise*. But really, we should read it as: Today you'll be *with me* in paradise.

Being with Jesus is the definition of paradise! The thing that makes paradise wonderful—the thing that makes paradise paradise—is the presence of Jesus. It's not paradise primarily because there are a lot of fun things to do and see. It's not paradise primarily because the problems that plague you here on earth are behind you. It's not even paradise primarily because the people you loved most and who had faith in Jesus will be there. It's paradise because you will be with Jesus.

This is a whole different way to look at our future, and our life in the present. It's what Paul is getting at in Philippians 1 v 23. He's writing from prison, and facing the real possibility of execution. How does he react? Not like the first criminal on the cross, railing at Jesus for landing him in jail. Not focusing on his present problems. What does he want? "I desire to depart and be with Christ, which is better by far."

What does Paul want? To be in heaven. Not sitting in a mansion in the sky, or lining up at an endless buffet, but with Jesus.

Don't miss this: Jesus is the hope of heaven. Jesus is the promise. He is the reward. Ultimately, that's the difference between those two thieves. The first wants Jesus to do things for him. The second just wants Jesus. The first will love Jesus if He gives him what he demands right now. The second just wants Jesus to remember him, to know him, beyond death.

It's worth asking ourselves: if heaven gave me everything— the job, the girl or guy, the car, the health, the wealth—but Jesus wasn't there, would I be content there? Or if heaven gave me nothing except Jesus, would I be satisfied? Deep down, I think I often answer "yes" and "no". That's because I love other things too much, and I love the Lord Jesus far, far too little.

Now, the point here is not to heap guilt and condemnation on ourselves. That's exactly the opposite of the point. The point is that we take all of our false and pathetic loves to Jesus and we find that He died for even those sins. He died to take away the guilt for our shamefully weak and misdirected passions and desires. He died so that we are forgiven for loving what He gives us more than we love Him. And so when we go to Him, we don't find him angry and scolding. We find Him gracious and forgiving, with the power to help us change.

We need to focus on our future more than our present. We need to love our Lord more than we love anything else in our lives. We need to yearn for heaven, simply because that is where we will be with Jesus. How can we do this? Look at Jesus' passion, what He did for you, and you will find yourself growing passionate about Him. As you meditate on Jesus' love and humility and all that He did for you, your love for Him will be stoked into a blaze that dwarfs anything else. As you look at the dazzling beauty of His honesty, His humility, His integrity and His sacrifice, other things will pale in comparison.

Then you'll become like that second criminal. He only wanted to be with Jesus. Let the same be true of us.

For Reflection:

- *Do you ever set God conditions for following Him? How?*
- *Whose actions do you rely on to reach heaven: yours, or the Lord's? What difference does this make to your confidence of reaching paradise?*
- *How can you become more excited about seeing Jesus? What are the other things in your life that you could most easily love more than Him?*

The sands of time are sinking, the dawn of Heaven breaks;
The summer morn I've sighed for—the fair, sweet morn
    awakes:
Dark, dark hath been the midnight, but dayspring is at
    hand,
And glory—glory dwelleth in Immanuel's land.

Soon shall the cup of glory wash down earth's bitterest
    woes,
Soon shall the desert briar break into Eden's rose;
The curse shall change to blessing, the name on earth that's
    banned
Be graven on the white stone in Immanuel's land.

Oh! I am my Beloved's and my Beloved is mine!
He brings a poor vile sinner into His "house of wine."
I stand upon His merit—I know no other stand,
Not even where glory dwelleth in Immanuel's land.

The Bride eyes not her garment, but her dear Bridegroom's
    face;
I will not gaze at glory but on my King of grace.
Not at the crown He gifteth but on His piercèd hand;
The Lamb is all the glory of Immanuel's land.

"The Sands of Time are Sinking" by Anne R. Cousin

CHAPTER NINE

CLIMAX

I ⁴⁴ It was now about the sixth hour, and darkness came over the whole land until the ninth hour, ⁴⁵ for the sun stopped shining. And the curtain of the temple was torn in two. ⁴⁶ Jesus called out with a loud voice, "Father, into your hands I commit my spirit." When he had said this, he breathed his last.

⁴⁷ The centurion, seeing what had happened, praised God and said, "Surely this was a righteous man." ⁴⁸ When all the people who had gathered to witness this sight saw what took place, they beat their breasts and went away. ⁴⁹ But all those who knew him, including the women who had followed him from Galilee, stood at a distance, watching these things.

⁵⁰ Now there was a man named Joseph, a member of the Council, a good and upright man, ⁵¹ who had not consented to their decision and action. He came from the Judean town of Arimathea and he was waiting for the kingdom of God. ⁵² Going to Pilate, he asked for Jesus' body. ⁵³ Then he took it down, wrapped it in linen cloth and placed it in a tomb cut in the rock, one in which no one had yet been laid.

Luke 23 v 44-53

These events are the center of the Bible, the center of human history, and the center of the Christian faith.

Everything that had ever happened before was building up to this moment. Back in Genesis, after Adam and Eve had rebelled against God and brought the curse of death and condemnation on themselves, God promised them that one of their descendants would destroy Satan, even though Satan would "bruise his heel" (Genesis 3 v 15).

Then God called Abraham to trust Him and live for Him, and promised to bring blessing to the nations through the family of this childless man (Genesis 12 v 1-3). Abraham's descendants grew into a great people, and God led them out of slavery in Egypt and into the promised land. There, He gave them kings to rule them, the greatest of whom was King David. He promised David that one of his line would be a King who would rule for ever.

Hundreds of years later, despite the people going off into exile because of their persistent rebellion, His messenger Isaiah saw the coming day of a righteous servant of God, who would bear the sins of God's people. Through all the prophets, God repeatedly reassured His people that He had not forgotten His promises: that His King, His servant, His serpent-crushing blessing-bringer would come.

All of that history is being brought to a head here, in these verses. This is God's plan to destroy Satan and deliver His people from their sins, so that they can be blessed and enjoy life as it was meant to be. It has all come down to this moment.

And so everything that has happened from this moment forward is transformed by it. From this point on, nothing is the same in the world or in the lives of God's people. After Jesus dies and is raised, His followers become a force to be reckoned with, turning the world upside down without weapons or force. The whole New Testament is an unpacking of the implications of Jesus' death. It's all commentary on the cross.

These are the most important hours in human history.

The Darkness

Jesus is crucified at "the sixth hour" (v 44): noon, the time when the sun is at its peak and the daylight is the brightest. And yet "darkness came over the whole land ... for the sun stopped shining" (v 44-45). Instead of bright sunshine, everything is enveloped in three hours of sudden and miraculous pitch-black darkness.

What is the meaning of this darkness? If you look over the Bible, you see that darkness can mean three things (other than simply that it's night-time!). First, the authors of the scriptures use the concept of darkness to describe shameful, wicked deeds. Evil men "walk in dark ways" (Proverbs 2 v 13) and rebels against God "sat in darkness" (Psalm 107 v 10-11). Paul says Christians should:

> have nothing to do with the fruitless deeds of darkness, but rather
> expose them. For it is shameful even to mention what the disobedi-
> ent do in secret.   (Ephesians 5 v 11-12)

"Darkness" represents a time when people can do shameful things without fear of being seen or known. And the whole of the last day of Jesus' life—His betrayal and arrest, His trial and torture, and now His execution—are dark deeds, when human evil seems to prevail. It is, as Jesus told His enemies, "your hour—when darkness reigns" (Luke 22 v 53). So it's appropriate that this most shameful deed of all, the murder of the Messiah, is cloaked in darkness.

Second, darkness denotes anti-God forces. Even at creation, this is pictured powerfully as God speaks into the darkness and the chaos, and creates... light! (Genesis 1 v 2-3). God's spiritual enemies are described as "the powers of this dark world" (Ephesians 6 v 12), and the reign of His most powerful opponent, Satan, is pictured as the "dominion of darkness" (Colossians 1 v 13). God, on the other hand, "is light; in him there is no darkness at all" (1 John 1 v 5).

So there is a sense in which the darkness surrounding Jesus on the cross represents the momentary triumph of evil. All through history, Satan had been trying to prevent the coming of the Messiah. When God's Son Jesus appeared, he focused all his efforts on stopping Him. He motivated Herod (the father of Herod Antipas, who we met earlier) to murder all the baby boys in Bethlehem. He tempted Jesus with the riches and respect of the world. He sent his spiritual forces into men and women who lay in the Son of God's path.

None of these had stopped Jesus. But here, now, Satan has finally done it. The Messiah is dying, and will soon be dead, defeated by the forces of darkness. Or so it seems, for those three hours.

Third, darkness in the Bible can represent judgment from God. The penultimate plague He sent on Egypt in Exodus 10 was total darkness in the land. And when His prophets spoke of the future day when God would finally judge all sin, they pictured it as a day of darkness:

> Let all who live in the land tremble, for the day of the LORD is
> coming. It is close at hand—a day of darkness and gloom, a day of
> clouds and blackness!
>
> (Joel 2 v 1-2; look also at Amos 5 v 18-20 and Ezekiel 32 v 7-8)

Human evil; spiritual rebellion; God's judgment. The darkness which surrounds the dying Christ could be indicators of any of those three. And in fact, it's an indicator of all of those three. As we combine those three streams of meaning, it's easy to see that these three hours of darkness are quite significant. This is a shameful, wicked deed. This looks like the victory of Satan and evil. And this is also a place where God is judging sin and rebellion against Him in His world.

So when the darkness lifts, we'd expect that God's judgment will have fallen on the people who are killing His Son. But when the light returns, only one person has experienced God's wrath: His own Son. Jesus was plunged into the deep spiritual darkness. He hung there, suspended between heaven and earth, abandoned by His friends, destroyed by His enemies... and punished by His Father.

This is the most shocking aspect of the darkness around the cross. For the first, last and only time in eternity, God the Father and God the Son were not in perfect relationship. God the Father looked at Jesus, His Son with whom He'd always been "well pleased" (Luke 3 v 22), who He'd always loved (Mark 9 v 7); and He punished Him. He excluded Him from His presence and His pleasure. The darkness in the sky reflected the state of the relationship between Father and Son. For Jesus, the Son of God, the cross was utter, utter darkness.

Why did this have to happen? The rest of the New Testament shows us what Jesus accomplished as He hung in that darkness:

> You are a chosen people ... a people belonging to God, that you may declare the praises of him who called you out of darkness into his wonderful light. Once you were not a people, but now you are the people of God; once you had not received mercy, but now you have received mercy. (1 Peter 2 v 9-10)

On the cross, Jesus experienced darkness so that we might never know a minute of it. Jesus experienced the bone-shattering, soul-rending terror of rejection from God, of separation from all God's blessings, so that we might never need to. And not only did He take away the darkness we earned for ourselves, He won for us the eternal light of God's loving presence in our lives.

If you are a follower of Jesus, when you look at Him on the cross, enveloped in darkness both physical and spiritual, you should see that He was taking what you deserve. That is your darkness, your shame, and your grief, because that is your sin. And when you read in Revelation of an eternal future where God's people "will not need the light of a lamp or the light of the sun, for the Lord God will give them light" (22 v 5), you should see that Jesus has given you what He deserves. That is His glory, His perfection, and His joy, given to you.

What a Savior!

The Final Sacrifice

At the cross, the darkness of human rebellion, spiritual evil and divine judgment came together so that in the future we need never face any of them. And at the cross, another ancient theme was climaxing, too: sacrifice.

Ever since humanity lost its place in Eden, the way to approach and remain in relationship with God has been through sacrifice. In Genesis 3, Adam and Eve's children, Cain and Abel, offered sacrifices. Right after Noah got out of the ark in Genesis 9, he sacrificed an animal to the LORD. All of the patriarchs—Abraham, Isaac, and Jacob—made sacrifices. But it was when the people of Israel received the law of God that He gave them a very specific, detailed plan for sacrifices. And one particular sacrifice stood out as being central in the life of Israel: *Yom Kippur*, the Day of Atonement. It's detailed in Leviticus 16.

On this one day each year, the high priest of Israel would take a bath, put on a special white linen outfit, and choose a bull as a sacrifice for his sins and the sins of his family. He would then cast lots over two goats, selecting one as a sacrifice to God and one as a "scapegoat". Next, the high priest would sacrifice the bull for his own sins, and then go into the Most Holy Place, the part of the tabernacle (later the temple in Jerusalem) where God dwelled among His people in all His purity. It was the holiest place in the world. The high priest would sprinkle the blood of the bull in the Most Holy Place, and then sacrifice the goat and do the same thing.

After that, he would mix the blood of the bull and the goat together and put it on the altar outside the Most Holy Place, in order to cleanse it from the sins of the people. Then the high priest would put his hands on the head of the remaining goat and confess all the sins of Israel, transferring them to the goat. The goat would then be led off into the wilderness, a sign that the people's sins had been taken far away.

The symbolism of these sacrifices was not particularly obscure or complex. "Here's what your sins deserve", the Day of Atonement said to the people as the priest stabbed a bull in the neck. Subtlety was not a virtue in this case.

It is simple. Terrifying, but simple. Sin always results in death. Blood is a symbol of life; it's literally our life-blood. And so if sin brings death but you want to be forgiven and not have to pay the ultimate price for your sin, something is going to have to die in your place. There can be no forgiveness without blood being shed. The sacrificial system that God gave Israel was a brutal reminder of that reality. Sin brings death. Forgiveness requires sacrifice.

But the destruction wreaked by sin wasn't limited to the sentence of death. It also caused human beings to be separated from God. After their sin, Adam and Eve were cast out of the Garden of Eden and no longer enjoyed face-to-face fellowship with their Creator. At the entrance to His presence in Eden, God placed angels with a flashing sword (Genesis 3 v 24). Imperfect humanity was separated from God's presence.

This separation was pictured vividly in the temple. Everything about the design of the temple was there to make clear that God was unapproachable—that sinners simply could not live with God. Sometimes people talk about God as if He's a cosmic blend of your grandpa and Santa Claus, an old man who is content to see you once a year and lives to shower you with gifts. But God is nothing like that; He is perfectly holy and perfectly just, He sets perfect standards, and He is a consuming fire to those who fail to meet them (Hebrews 12 v 29).

So in front of the Most Holy Place was a thick, heavy curtain, embroidered with angels (Exodus 36 v 35). Its message was stark: "You can't come near God. In fact, you shouldn't even look in here at God." It said to sinners: "Danger! Keep Out!" Like a fence that keeps you from entering a high-voltage area, the curtain was a warning.

If you were a normal Israelite, you could never come closer to God's presence than the outer courtyard of the tabernacle. If you were a priest and you were lucky, you could enter into the Holy Place, the area around the Most Holy Place, for one week out of your life. But even as a priest, for just one week, you were still separated by the curtain. Only if you were named the high priest for a year could you spend a few amazing minutes in your whole life in God's presence-on-earth.

That was it.

The message of the sacrifices and the curtain was clear: sin brings death and separation from God. For centuries, hundreds of thousands of Israelites made sacrifice at the temple. Thousands of priests served in the temple. Far fewer high priests went behind the curtain, once, briefly, after all the washing and sacrificing demanded in Leviticus 16. And all the time, the temple curtain hung there, a huge Keep Out sign.

Until one day, "the curtain of the temple was torn in two" (Luke 23 v 45). This was no small thing; the curtain was thirty feet by thirty feet and a whole inch thick. No man could have ripped it without a sharp sword, a long ladder, and a lot of time. But no man did rip it; this was a divine tearing, God's way of showing that the way to His presence was now open to sinners.

Why did it tear? Because on a cross only a few hundred yards from the temple, the final sacrifice had been made. Jesus' death was the sacrifice to end all sacrifice. The blood of a goat or a bull couldn't truly, completely remove sin. How could a mindless goat pay the price for our conscious, willful rebellion against the Creator of the universe? That goat wasn't morally pure; it wasn't even aware of what was happening to it.

But Jesus was. Luke is very concerned to show us that Jesus was a righteous, willing sacrifice. In verse 46 He commits His spirit into the Father's hands; He willingly lays down His life. And then the centurion overseeing this death, "seeing what had happened, praised God and said, 'Surely this was a righteous man'" (v 47). This is a hardened pagan executioner; who knows how many people he has crucified? But as he watches Jesus die, calling out to the Father for the forgiveness of His tormentors, pardoning the thief next to Him and finally giving up His life, this man is changed. He praises God and proclaims Jesus' perfect innocence.

Jesus is the willing and ultimate sacrifice. He was fully God and the fully perfect man. And so His sacrifice is of infinite worth, and never needs to be repeated. Think of all the animals that had been sacrificed in the tabernacle and temple, day after day and year after year. Put it all together and theirs would be a river of blood, a symbol of endless sacrifice and guilt that is never finally dealt with. But now, Jesus enters the darkness, sacrifices His life, and the temple curtain is ripped in two.

All the sacrifices through all the ages have been pointing to this moment; and now no more blood needs to be shed. Through Christ, we have direct access to God:

> We have confidence to enter the Most Holy Place by the blood of Jesus, by a new and living way opened for us through the curtain.
>
> (Hebrews 10 v 19-20)

Before, access to God was limited and partial and fearful. Now, Christ's sacrifice has torn open the curtain. The way has been opened for the dying thief next to Jesus to enjoy God's presence for ever, instead of enduring separation from Him eternally. And it has been opened for us, too.

Standing for Christ

But at the time, this simply looked like just another execution. And so Jesus "breathed his last" (Luke 23 v 46), just as all crucified men did sooner or later. And the crowd, just as they always did, "beat their breasts and went away" (v 48), leaving only Jesus' closest friends watching from a distance. The show was over. The man was dead.

Then along came "a man named Joseph" (v 50). This is the first time in the whole Gospel that we've heard of him. This Joseph is a fairly powerful man. He is a member of the

Sanhedrin, the Council of Jewish leaders, and he evidently has enough pull to gain an audience with Pilate. And he is also a good man. He "had not consented" to the council's decision and action in condemning Jesus.

In fact, Joseph has made a very different decision to them. "He was waiting for the kingdom of God" (v 51)—which seems to be Luke's way of saying Joseph is a follower of Jesus.

Oftentimes, the bodies of crucified men would be left up on the cross to rot away and serve as a warning to potential criminals; so Joseph goes to Pilate and ask for permission to spare Jesus' body that indignity. Pilate, perhaps eager to try to ease his guilty conscience, grants his request and Joseph has Him buried in his own private (as yet unused) family tomb.

It's easy to allow Joseph to become an insignificant footnote in the larger story of the crucifixion. But he actually occupies a position of privilege in Luke's narrative. His is the first response to Jesus' death that we're shown in any great detail; his kindness is the first act of discipleship that we see after Jesus' death. And so Joseph serves as a picture of how to respond faithfully to the reality of the death of Christ.

Joseph reminds us that there is a certain amount of courage required of anyone who would be Jesus' follower. His is an act of tremendous bravery; John 19 v 38 tells us that up until this point, Joseph has kept his respect for Jesus a secret out of fear of the Jewish rulers. In going to Pilate, he is taking a risk; this isn't a good time to be identified with Jesus. He is giving up his reputation; this isn't an action his fellow Council members are likely to applaud. And he is taking a financial hit; tombs were not cheap, and so were the preserve of the wealthy.

Joseph is standing with Jesus when almost everyone around him has turned against Him. And to be honest, it all seems a little pointless. What good is it to make sure Jesus' body is buried? What difference will that possibly make? The dream is over—the Christ is dead!

And yet God uses Joseph's act of devotion in a way he could never have imagined. That donated tomb will become the scene of one of the most wonderful events in human history, as Jesus is raised from the grave.

Christians are willing to stand with Jesus even when the tide of popular opinion is against Him; even when it requires a risk to our reputation or bank balance or even safety; and even when it may not seem to make much difference. In many places around the world, publicly identifying with Christ might cost a believer their family, their job, even their life. For Christians in the west, following Jesus might cost someone their reputation, their promotion, or their friendships.

While those costs are significant, the response of faith is to prefer suffering with Christ to ease and pleasure in this world. As Jesus taught:

> Whoever wants to save his life will lose it, but whoever loses his life for me will save it. What good is it for a man to gain the whole world, and yet lose or forfeit his very self? If anyone is ashamed of me and my words, the Son of Man will be ashamed of him when he comes in his glory and in the glory of the Father and of the holy angels.
>
> (Luke 9 v 24-26)

It's short-sighted to choose the good opinion of other men and women over courageous faithfulness to Christ.

At different times and in different ways we will all have Joseph's choice presented to us: will we risk standing with Jesus whatever the consequences, or will we play it safe? You may live in a place where doing this may very easily cost you your life. And if you live somewhere where it is unlikely to, the smaller interactions of your workaday lives will be the arena in which you have the chance and the challenge of preferring loving loyalty to Christ over the comforts of the world. It can be very intimidating to identify with Jesus (in word and deed) in a neighborhood mother's group or a factory break room or in the locker room at the gym. But those are the places God has given us to let our reputation die in order to be loyal to Him. If we're really willing to die for Jesus, we'll be willing to risk anything else for Him.

After all, the worst that can happen is death: and death holds no fear for the Christian. There is no darkness; there is no separation. We can die as Jesus did, saying: "Father, into your hands I commit my spirit" (23 v 46).

Jesus did not die in panic and terror, but after His intense suffering He entrusted His death to His Father. Jesus knew that after He endured the cross, there was joy set before Him, the joy of being seated at His Father's right hand (Hebrews 12 v 2). For Christians, death may seem untimely, feel painful, appear tragic; but we can die peacefully as people who know we are going to be with the Lord, the Lord who hung in the darkness so that we can live in eternal light with Him. And when a man or woman is not afraid to die, they are free to live for Christ.

For Reflection:

- *Jesus took **your** darkness. How does that make you feel?*
- *As you look towards your own death, how do the events of this passage encourage and comfort you?*
- *What opportunities has God given you in your life to be loyal to Jesus in the way Joseph was?*

Alas! and did my Savior bleed
And did my Sovereign die?
Would He devote that sacred head
For such a worm as I?

Was it for crimes that I had done
He groaned upon the tree?
Amazing pity! Grace unknown!
And love beyond degree!

Well might the sun in darkness hide
And shut his glories in,
When Christ, the mighty Maker died,
For man the creature's sin.

Thus might I hide my blushing face
While His dear cross appears,
Dissolve my heart in thankfulness,
And melt my eyes to tears.

But drops of grief can ne'er repay
The debt of love I owe:
Here, Lord, I give myself away,
Tis all that I can do.

"At the Cross" by Isaac Watts

CHAPTER TEN

ANOTHER DAY

I

[54] It was Preparation Day, and the Sabbath was about to begin.

[55] The women who had come with Jesus from Galilee followed Joseph and saw the tomb and how his body was laid in it. [56] Then they went home and prepared spices and perfumes. But they rested on the Sabbath in obedience to the commandment.

[1] On the first day of the week, very early in the morning, the women took the spices they had prepared and went to the tomb. [2] They found the stone rolled away from the tomb, [3] but when they entered, they did not find the body of the Lord Jesus. [4] While they were wondering about this, suddenly two men in clothes that gleamed like lightning stood beside them. [5] In their fright the women bowed down with their faces to the ground, but the men said to them, "Why do you look for the living among the dead? [6] He is not here; he has risen! Remember how he told you, while he was still with you in Galilee: [7] 'The Son of Man must be delivered into the hands of sinful men, be crucified and on the third day be raised again.'" [8] Then they remembered his words.

[9] When they came back from the tomb, they told all these things to the Eleven and to all the others. [10] It was Mary Magdalene, Joanna, Mary the mother of James, and the others with them who told this to the apostles. [11] But they did not believe the women, because their words seemed to them like nonsense. [12] Peter, however, got up and ran to the tomb. Bending over, he saw the strips of linen lying by themselves, and he went away, wondering to himself what had happened.   Luke 23 v 54 – 24 v 12

Lord of the Rings author J.R.R. Tolkien once noted that in our best stories there is a "ring of truth"; something that echoes the great reality described in the Bible. The Bible tells a story about the world that we live in. It's a true story of a glorious creation, a terrible rebellion, and the lengths to which God went to put things right again. That's the story that we all live in and that shapes our reality.

Have you ever noticed that almost every great, epic story moves along that same basic plot structure? The story begins at some happy time in a situation that you wish could last forever. Then comes a problem which threatens that early happiness; some villain comes on the scene and presents a difficulty. Next a hero emerges to solve the problem, and we get caught up in their success as they begin to put things right. But then the hero experiences some huge setback and it looks as though evil will prevail, until there is some unforeseen twist, the hero emerges victorious, and everyone lives "happily ever after".

We love those stories because they resonate with what we sense to be true, or what we sense ought to be true, about our world. Every day, we're presented with fragments of that overarching story: the longing for happiness; the reality of problems, pain and disappointment; the yearning for a happy ending.

Together, we have traced part of the story of Luke's Gospel. We have seen our hero (Jesus, if you've not been paying attention) come into a fallen world, broken by sin, and take on the forces of darkness and evil. Yet as Jesus hung on the cross, the victim of His enemies' political maneuvers, the great hope now expending His final breath, it must have looked to His followers as though the tale was finished and all was lost.

But thankfully, the story isn't over yet.

Back from the Dead

Normally, there was an elaborate process for preparing a body for burial, using spices and ointments and a linen shroud. But Jesus died on a Friday afternoon, and the Sabbath—the day of rest—began at sundown on Friday evening. People would take time on Friday to prepare their food and get things in order so that they wouldn't have to work on the Sabbath.

All of which meant that the people who wanted to bury Jesus didn't have much time. Jewish custom forbade this kind of activity on the Sabbath, and so Jesus' body only received half the attention it would normally have received. The faithful women who had been with Jesus noted the location of the tomb and went home to prepare the spices. Their plan was to wait until after the Sabbath was over and then, as soon as it was light on Sunday, go and try to find someone to move the stone at the entrance so that they could properly prepare the body.

But when Sunday comes and they go to the tomb, they find three things that perplex and terrify them. The huge stone that sealed the tomb's entrance has been rolled away. Jesus' body is gone. And there are two men in shining clothing—angels—standing there at the entrance to the tomb. These messengers address the confusion of the women with seven simple words that change the world and which take us into the final chapter of this greatest of stories: "He is not here; he has risen!" (v 6).

Then they remind the women that Jesus had told them all about this: "Remember how he told you that he would be handed over to sinful men and be crucified and then rise on the third day?"

It's as if they're asking: "Do you notice any similarities between what Jesus predicted and the events of the last thirty-six hours?!" Finally the penny drops and the women understand: this was the plan all along.

Christians have a huge interest in this account of the resurrection being a historical event: we're staking our eternal future on it. Non-Christians have an equally huge vested interest in it not being historical: they're staking their eternal future on it. Every single person rests their entire eternal destiny on being correct in their understanding of Christ's resurrection.

So people have tried to come up with a number of alternative explanations for these events. It might have been a look-alike on the cross. Maybe some of the disciples stole Jesus' body and claimed that He was raised from the dead. Perhaps Jesus wasn't really dead, but had passed out from the pain of the cross. And so on.

But none of those theories fit with the testimony of the people who were actually there. Take the "look-alike" theory. Where did this look-alike come from? Can we really believe that Jesus' disciples, and even His own mother, wouldn't be able to see that it wasn't really Jesus on the cross? That they didn't recognize that His voice was different?

Or how about the "stolen body" theory? Would you be willing to spend your entire life in danger and poverty to spread a story that you knew wasn't true, being laughed at, rejected, arrested and even killed? If this theory is correct, that's exactly what the disciples did. What would be their motivation if they knew that they had stolen the body?

But the worst of all the alternative explanations is the "Jesus didn't really die" theory. The soldiers who reported back to Pilate in Mark 15 v 44 confirmed that Jesus was really dead; and usually soldiers are pretty good at making sure they've killed the people they are supposed to kill. They even jabbed a spear into His side for good measure.

All of the disciples understood that Jesus was really dead. The crowds went home beating their breasts in sorrow. The women who stood at the foot of the cross went back home to get ready to prepare the corpse. Joseph went to get a tomb ready. Everyone who was there agreed that He was dead. This is pretty indisputable.

And then, three days after Jesus died, He wasn't dead anymore. His tomb was unoccupied. The angels at the tomb said that He was alive. His disciples claimed that they saw Him and even ate breakfast with Him (John 21 v 4-14); and they lived the rest of their lives like men who had seen their teacher living after He had died.

On Friday, Jesus was really dead; on Sunday, He was really alive. Any deviation from these two facts gets you off into unconvincing fantasy and vain faith. This is why Paul wrote to the church in Corinth:

> I want to remind you of the gospel I preached to you, which you received and on which you have taken your stand. By this gospel you are saved, if you hold firmly to the word I preached to you. Otherwise, you have believed in vain. For what I received I passed on to you as of first importance: that Christ died for our sins according to the Scriptures, that he was buried, that he was raised on the third day according to the Scriptures. (1 Corinthians 15 v 1-4)

Your Story

If you've ever had your imagination captured by a great book, you know the bittersweet feeling that comes when you finally come to the end of the story. There's a sense of loss that you'll no longer be able to spend time with the characters that you've grown to love; a sense in which you long for the world of the book to be real, to be able to actually live your life in the universe created by the story.

If you are a Christian, Jesus' resurrection fulfills all those desires. Because He is alive and not dead, you actually *do* live in this story! All of the events described really happened, and all the characters you love are real—you'll meet them one day. Every part of the Christian life is shaped and empowered by the resurrection of the crucified Christ.

Let's walk through three ways in which the resurrection changes everything. This is a treasure chest for us; prepare to be dazzled by how awesome all of this is. Don't just read the words; gaze at their meaning. This is great news that will change not only the way you live tomorrow morning as you go to work or drop the kids off at school, but also the way you spend all of eternity.

Never-ending Life

First, because Jesus rose from the dead, you are saved from eternal death, for eternal life.

Without the resurrection, there is absolutely no salvation. Jesus hung on the cross in agony, shame, and condemnation. If that's the end of the story, then Jesus' death is nothing more than, at best, an example of self-sacrificing love. Inspiring, perhaps, but futile and ultimately useless. But the resurrection is an act of God the Father vindicating His Son (Acts 2 v 22-24), showing that His sacrifice for our sins is acceptable and good. It is Jesus' victory over sin and death, and it secures our forgiveness and right standing with God (Romans 4 v 25).

Having faith in Christ means staking your entire eternal destiny on Him. You say, in effect: "Where He went, I want to go". Your life depends on Him having been raised from the dead. But if you don't put your faith in Christ, you are saying that Jesus didn't rise from the dead, and if you are wrong, the consequences are disastrous.

When you die, you will face God and answer for the way that you have lived your life. If you stand on your own record, you will face God's wrath against you. But because Jesus defeated death by rising from the grave, our record can be replaced with His so that we can be welcomed into the presence of God. The resurrection is a demonstration of God's delight in His Son; and since we are Jesus' brothers and sisters, God delights in us, too. Our faith is not in vain!

Jesus' resurrection also means that we have a certain hope of future bodily resurrection. Jesus wasn't raised as a disembodied spirit—He had a glorified, physical body. He was able to tell His followers to "touch me and see; a ghost does not have flesh and bones, as you see I have" (Luke 24 v 39). He was able to sit and eat with them (v 43).

Now that our sin has been dealt with, there is nothing left to keep Jesus' people in our burial plots. Jesus declares:

> I was dead, and behold I am alive forever and ever! And I hold the keys of death and Hades. (Revelation 1 v 18)

Stop and read that again; look at what Jesus is saying. Because He was dead but is now alive, He has the keys to death. He has the authority; He calls the shots; death listens to Him.

If you're with Jesus, you are coming out of your grave someday to receive a glorified body, no longer subject to sin, decay and death. What Jesus has, you will have. You will be made alive just as He has been. The promise of the resurrection for Christ's people is that death will be swallowed up in victory, its sting will be removed, and the grave will not be the end. Jesus is the resurrection and the life, and because we are His we will live with Him for ever, in a real, physical, perfected existence.

Take a minute to read these promises from the New Testament. Slow down and try to understand what each means. Take time to believe that these things are true:

If we have been united with him like this in his death, we will certainly also be united with him in his resurrection. (Romans 6 v 5)

We believe that Jesus died and rose again and so we believe that God will bring with Jesus those who have fallen asleep in him.

(1 Thessalonians 4 v 14)

By his power God raised the Lord from the dead, and he will raise us also. (1 Corinthians 6 v 14)

Free to Live Life

Second, Christians don't live merely for the moment.

We don't need to live as if we must get everything we want right now, because otherwise we'll never know joy or happiness. We don't hedge our bets; we don't diversify our joy portfolio; all of our eggs are in one basket. As the apostle Paul said, it's all or nothing:

If only for this life we have hope in Christ, we are to be pitied more than all men. But Christ has indeed been raised from the dead...

(1 Corinthians 15 v 19-20)

So the question is: do you live this way? Do you live as if this life is all that you're going to get? Or do you live in light of the eternal life that you will have with Christ?

Here's how Paul described his life in a later letter that he wrote to this same church at Corinth:

Five times I received from the Jews the forty lashes minus one. Three times I was beaten with rods, once I was stoned, three times I was shipwrecked, I spent a night and a day in the open sea, I have been constantly on the move. I have been in danger from rivers, in danger from bandits, in danger from my own countrymen, in danger from Gentiles; in danger in the city, in danger in the country, in danger at sea; and in danger from false brothers. I have labored and toiled and have often gone without sleep; I have known hunger and thirst and have often gone without food; I have been cold and naked.   (2 Corinthians 11 v 24-27)

Does that sound like a good life to you?! Paul says that if Christ wasn't raised, his life has been lived for a lie and he has utterly wasted it. He has taken beatings and danger and endured hunger and cold, all for nothing. He is the most pitiful man ever, a pathetic fool.

But if Jesus rose from the dead, he has spent his life (literally) on the only thing that is eternally worthwhile; and he's been looking forward to eternity all the while.

Like Paul, we should live our lives as if we really believe what we say we believe. We should be so dependent on the reality of a future resurrection with Christ, have so much staked on this story, that if it were not true our lives would have been a total waste.

If you don't really think that Jesus rose from the dead, then you should eat, drink and be merry, because this is all you're going to get. And if you do live your life in the present, for the present, then it suggests that, deep down, you don't actually believe Jesus rose from the grave to give you life beyond it.

But since He did rise from the dead, we are free to really live life. We don't need to stuff ourselves with selfish pleasures here on earth. We are free to give our lives away as the apostle Paul did. We are free to live lives of self-sacrificing joy. We are free to pour out our lives, our time, our talent, our resources, into things that will have eternal value. We are free to meet with suffering or disaster or defeat and look beyond them. We are free to enjoy success and circumstances without wishing for more or worrying we'll lose them. We do not need to come to the end of our lives and say: "This was all a waste".

Jesus: With us through Life

The third implication for our lives is that because Jesus was raised from the dead, we have an ever-present Savior.

That might seem obvious, but all the best truths are. Jesus is alive, and so He is with us now. Christians are not worshipping a dead man; we're not following the writings of a dead philosopher. The power of Jesus isn't merely in His words or ideas, but in His presence.

Because Jesus is alive, He is able to send His Spirit to His followers, so that they can be "clothed with power from on high" (Luke 24 v 49). He is actually present in us by His Spirit, which empowers us with resurrection power (Romans 8 v 11). The very same might that ripped open the tomb and brought Jesus back from death is now at work in us and for us.

Nothing could keep Jesus in the grave, so great was the power of His resurrection; not the stone that had been rolled across the entrance, not the Roman soldiers, not the weight of our sin, not even the combined forces of hell. That's the power that enables us to stand up under suffering, persecution, and temptation. That's the power that enables us to live for Christ and live like Christ today.

Not only is the risen Christ present with us by His Spirit, but He has also ascended into heaven, where He lives to speak to His Father on His people's behalf (Hebrews 7 v 25). We never go through life alone and unobserved. Our struggles, our weaknesses, our temptations, our fear, loneliness, and anxieties are all seen by our ever-present Savior. We go through life with a friend who loved us enough to die for us and who is so strong that death couldn't hold Him. We know that, whatever happens, Jesus stands in heaven and speaks to God about us, saying: "Father, forgive". That makes all the difference.

In a way, this chapter doesn't really fit in this book. If we are only looking at the last day of Jesus' life, then it would make sense to finish as the faithful women left the tomb on Friday afternoon. But because of the resurrection, Jesus' final day wasn't really His final day. Jesus has no final day— there is always another to enjoy. And for those of us who are trusting in Him, our death isn't our last day either!

If you are a Christian, this is the story you are living in, right now. It's a better story than *The Lord of the Rings* and *Harry Potter* combined. It's a story whose ending you know, and whose climax you'll one day enjoy. You may not know all the plot points from this moment on, but you can be certain that it will have a happy ending, because it did for Jesus.

The resurrection means that, like the disciples, you can go on your way in life, today and every day, "with great joy" (Luke 24 v 52). The Passion of Christ means that, like Paul, you can say with absolute confidence and great excitement:

"For me, to live is Christ and to die is gain."

(Philippians 1 v 21)

For Reflection:

- *How would you explain the historicity and the significance of the resurrection to someone else?*

- *What difference does the security of your eternal future make to your view of life today?*

- *In what ways has the Passion of Christ Jesus made you more passionate about loving, serving and following Him?*

Christ the Lord is risen today, Alleluia!
Sons of men and angels say, Alleluia!
Raise your joys and triumphs high, Alleluia!
Sing, ye heavens, and earth, reply, Alleluia!

Lives again our glorious King, Alleluia!
Where, O death, is now thy sting? Alleluia!
Once He died our souls to save, Alleluia!
Where thy victory, O grave? Alleluia!

Love's redeeming work is done, Alleluia!
Fought the fight, the battle won, Alleluia!
Death in vain forbids His rise, Alleluia!
Christ hath opened paradise, Alleluia!

Soar we now where Christ has led, Alleluia!
Following our exalted Head, Alleluia!
Made like Him, like Him we rise, Alleluia!
Ours the cross, the grave, the skies, Alleluia!

"Christ the Lord is Risen Today" by Charles Wesley

READING PLANS

This book picks up the narrative towards the end of a story—the chapters of the Gospel of Luke I'm focussing on here don't come in a vacuum. And in fact, I'd rather you read, thought about, grappled with and appreciated Luke's book than mine! So here are three different reading plans, to encourage you to spend time enjoying the Gospel of Luke, and seeing how Luke uses the Old Testament to explain what is happening in his account.

Since this is a book about the events of the first Good Friday, I've structured the plans so that they are either eight days long, lending themselves to being read in Easter Week; or 50 days long, so that you can use them throughout Lent. But, of course, you can use them in any other week or month-and-a-half during the year!

EIGHT-DAY PLANS

JESUS' LAST DAY IN FULL:

Sunday	22 v 7-46	Chapter One of this book
Monday	22 v 47-71	Chapters Two and Three
Tuesday	23 v 1-12	Chapter Four
Wednesday	23 v 13-25	Chapter Five
Thursday	23 v 26-31	Chapter Six
Friday	23 v 32-43	Chapters Seven and Eight
Saturday	23 v 44-56	Chapter Nine
Sunday	24 v 1-35	Chapter Ten

THE PASSION IN THE OLD TESTAMENT:

Sunday	Jeremiah 25 v 15-29 (see Luke 22 v 41 42)
Monday	Isaiah 52 v 13 – 53 v 9 (Luke 22 v 63)
Tuesday	Daniel 7 v 1-28 (Luke 23 v 69)
Wednesday	Hosea 10 v 1-15 (Luke 23 v 28-31)
Thursday	Psalm 22 v 1-21 (Luke 23 v 34-37)
Friday	Joel 2 v 1-11 (Luke 23 v 44-45a)
Saturday	Leviticus 16 (Luke 23 v 46b)
Sunday	Isaiah 53 v 10-12; Psalm 22 v 22-31 (Luke 24 v 6-7)

JESUS' LAST WEEK, DAY BY DAY:

Sunday	Luke 19 v 28-44
Monday	Luke 19 v 45-48
Tuesday	Luke 20 v 1 – 21 v 4
Wednesday	Luke 21 v 5-38
Thursday	Luke 22 v 7-54
Friday	Luke 22 v 55 – 23 v 55
Saturday	Luke 23 v 56
Sunday	Luke 24 v 1-49

FIFTY DAY PLAN—THROUGH THE GOSPEL OF LUKE:

1	1 v 1-38	27	13 v 31 – 14 v 14
	Ash Wednesday if	28	14 v 15-35
	reading through Lent	29	15 v 1-32
2	1 v 39-80	30	16 v 1-31
3	2 v 1-20	31	17 v 1-19
4	2 v 21-52	32	17 v 20 – 18 v 8
5	3 v 1-20	33	18 v 9-30
6	3 v 21 – 4 v 13	34	18 v 31 – 19 v 27
7	4 v 14-36	35	19 v 28-48
8	4 v 7 – 5 v 11	36	20 v 9-26
9	5 v 12-32	37	20 v 27 – 21 v 4
10	5 v 33 – 6 v 16	38	21 v 5-38
11	6 v 17-26	39	22 v 1-38
12	6 v 27-49	40	22 v 39-46
13	7 v 1-17		*Palm Sunday*
14	7 v 18-50	41	22 v 47-71
15	8 v 1-25	42	23 v 1-12
16	8 v 26-56	43	23 v 13-25
17	9 v 1-36	44	23 v 26-31
18	9 v 37-62	45	23 v 32-43
19	10 v 1-24		*Good Friday*
20	10 v 25-42	46	23 v 44-56
21	11 v 1-28	47	24 v 1-12
22	11 v 29-54		*Easter Sunday*
23	12 v 1-34	48	24 v 13-32
24	12 v 35-59	49	24 v 33-43
25	13 v 1-17	50	24 v 44-53
26	13 v 18-30		

ACKNOWLEDGEMENTS

This book has grown out of a series of sermons preached at Guilford Baptist Church, Virginia. The people of Guilford are wonderful hearers of God's word, and a delight to preach to week in and week out. It was very kind of them to give me the time to turn my sermon notes into a book.

I am also grateful for the hospitality that I enjoyed from Brian and Leslie Roe, John and Anne Casey, and Doris Aitken at different points in the process of writing this book.

I owe a debt of gratitude to The Good Book Company, especially to Brad Byrd for his faithful friendship, Tim Thornborough for his encouragement, and Carl Laferton for his significant editorial improvements to the manuscript. It is a pleasure to work with a group of people who delight so much in the Scriptures.

And finally, thanks to my family. Karen, my lovely wife, is a never-ending reservoir of support and patience, in addition to being my best friend. My kids, Kendall, Knox, Phineas, Ebenezer, and Harper give me so many reasons to smile every day, and this book is dedicated to them.

Other new titles from **thegoodbook**
<small>COMPANY</small>

The Hard Corps
by Dai Hankey

A gripping, powerful and startling retelling of the exploits of the Mighty Men who fought alongside King David. These are stories that shine a powerful and sometimes uncomfortable light on what it means to be a true man of God today. This is a no-holds-barred guide to spiritual warfare for today's Christian man.

"Faithful, missional and passionate. Pick up The Hard Corps and let the Spirit encourage and challenge you." **Matt Chandler**, Pastor of The Village Church, Flower Mound, Texas; President of Acts 29.

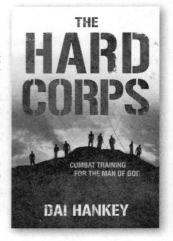

Compared to Her...
by Sophie de Witt

This warm, real and compelling book introduces you to the little-known but commonly-suffered "Compulsive Comparison Syndrome". Sophie shows how CCS causes envy, despair, pride and superiority; explains its causes; reveals how the gospel message treats it; and shows how women can move beyond it to live a life of true, lasting contentment.

"Accessible, jargon-free, and dealing with a struggle that women are very prone to. This is a really helpful book." **Kathy Keller**, co-author of *The Meaning of Marriage*.

Galatians For You
by Timothy Keller

The first in a brand-new ground-breaking series, Tim Keller brings his trademark insights and real-world applications to the book of Galatians. Written for Christians of every age and stage, whether new believers or pastors and teachers, this resource takes the reader through Galatians.

Galatians for You is for you:

- *to read* as a book, mapping out the themes and challenges of the epistle
- *to feed,* using it as a daily devotional, complete with helpful reflection questions
- *to lead,* equipping small-group leaders and Bible teachers and preachers to explain, illustrate and apply the wonderful book of the Bible.

Out spring 2013. Pre-order at www.thegoodbook.com (North America) or www.thegoodbook.co.uk (UK&Europe)

Timothy Keller is Senior Pastor of Redeemer Presbyterian Church in Manhattan, New York, and the bestselling author of titles such as *The Reason for God, The Meaning of Marriage* and *Counterfeit Gods*.

More from Mike McKinley: books...

Am I Really a Christian?
Jesus divided the world into two groups—those who follow him and those who don't. But what happens when someone thinks he or she is a Christian, but isn't? With his witty, engaging style, Mike takes readers on a journey of what it means to be a Christian.

Church Planting is For Wimps
An honest, realistic and at times hilarious look at church planting, stemming from Mike's successes and failures. This is a book which will inspire some people to become planters; encourage those who have planted; and challenge everyone to pray for church planting teams, whether or not they're a member of one.

Daily Bible-study…

Explore is a Bible-study devotional for your daily walk with God. Available as a book or as an app, *Explore* features Mike's notes on Proverbs and Jeremiah, alongside contributions from trusted teachers including Timothy Keller, Mark Dever, Graham Beynon, Tim Chester and Stephen Witmer.

Find out more at:

www.thegoodbook.com/explore

www.thegoodbook.co.uk/explore

thegoodbook
COMPANY
Opening up the Bible

At The Good Book Company, we are dedicated to helping Christians and local churches grow. We believe that God's growth process always starts with hearing clearly what He has said to us through His timeless word—the Bible.

Ever since we opened our doors in 1991, we have been striving to produce resources that honor God in the way the Bible is used. We have grown to become an international provider of user-friendly resources to the Christian community, with believers of all backgrounds and denominations using our Bible studies, books, evangelistic resources, DVD-based courses and training events.

We want to equip ordinary Christians to live for Christ day by day, and churches to grow in their knowledge of God, their love for one another, and the effectiveness of their outreach.

Call us for a discussion of your needs or visit one of our local websites for more information on the resources and services we provide.

N America: www.thegoodbook.com
UK & Europe: www.thegoodbook.co.uk
Australia: www.thegoodbook.com.au
New Zealand: www.thegoodbook.co.nz

N America: 866 244 2165
UK & Europe: 0333 123 0880
Australia: (02) 6100 4211
New Zealand (+64) 3 343 1990

www.christianityexplored.org

Our partner site is a great place for those exploring the Christian faith, with a clear explanation of the good news, powerful testimonies and answers to difficult questions.

One life. What's it all about?